73 CRIME & DETECTION
74 RUSSIA
75 LIGHT
76 ENERGY
77 ELECTRICITY
78 FORCE & MOTION
79 CHEMISTRY
80 MATTER
81 TIME & SPACE
82 ASTRONOMY
83 EARTH
84 LIFE
85 EVOLUTION
86 ECOLOGY
87 HUMAN BODY
88 MEDICINE
89 TECHNOLOGY
90 ELECTRONICS
91 RENAISSANCE
92 IMPRESSIONISM
93 GOYA
94 MANET
95 MONET
96 VAN GOGH
97 WATERCOLOR
98 PERSPECTIVE
99 DANCE
100 FUTURE
101 MYTHOLOGY
102 LEONARDO & HIS TIMES
103 OLYMPICS
104 MEDIA & COMMUNICATION
105 TITANIC
106 FOOTBALL
107 HURRICANE & TORNADO
108 SOCCER
109 PRESIDENTS
110 BASEBALL
111 EPIDEMIC
112 WORLD WAR II
113 SUPER BOWL
114 CIVIL WAR
115 RESCUE
116 EVEREST

DORLING KINDERSLEY **DK** EYEWITNESS BOOKS

OLYMPICS

Taking up a pose in a gymnastics floor exercise

60ᶠ OLYMPIA XVII. MAGYAR POSTA

Hungarian stamp commemorating the 1960 games in Rome

Athlete's outfit of the 1950s

Performing in a dressage event

Torch used in Seoul in 1988

Wheelchair racing

Warming up before training

DK EYEWITNESS BOOKS

OLYMPICS

Written by
CHRIS OXLADE
& DAVID BALLHEIMER

Pin commemorating the
1924 games in Paris

Dorling Kindersley

Dorling Kindersley

LONDON, NEW YORK, DELHI, JOHANNESBURG, MUNICH,
PARIS and SYDNEY

For a full catalog, visit

 www.dk.com

Commemorative
medal from the 1936
games in Berlin

Starting blocks

Javelin shoe

Running shoe

Sprint shoe

Project editor Louise Pritchard
Art editor Jill Plank
Senior managing editor Linda Martin
Senior managing art editor Julia Harris
Production Kate Oliver
Picture researcher Sean Hunter
DTP designer Andrew O'Brien
Photographers Andy Crawford, Bob Langrish,
and Steve Teague

This Eyewitness ® Book has been conceived by
Dorling Kindersley Limited
and Editions Gallimard

© 1999 Dorling Kindersley Limited
This edition © 2000
Dorling Kindersley Limited
First American edition, 1999

Published in the United States by
Dorling Kindersley Publishing, Inc.
95 Madison Avenue
New York, NY 10016
4 6 8 10 9 7 5

Dorling Kindersley books are available at special discounts for bulk
purchases for sales promotions or premiums. Special editions, including
personalized covers, excerpts of existing guides, and corporate imprints
can be created in large quantities for specific needs. For more information,
contact Special Markets Dept., Dorling Kindersley Publishing, Inc., 95
Madison Ave., New York, NY 10016; Fax: (800) 600-9098

Library of Congress Cataloging-in-Publication Data
Oxlade, Chris.
Olympics / written by Chris Oxlade.
p. cm. — (Eyewitness Books)
Includes index.
Summary: Surveys the history and traditions of the Olympics,
highlighting memorable events from ancient Greece
to the present day.
1. Olympics — Juvenile literature.
[1. Olympics — History.] I. Title. II. Series.
GV721.53.O95.   2000
796.48'09 — dc21   99–22807 CIP

ISBN 0-7894-6293-1 (pb)
ISBN 0-7894-6292-3 (hc)

Color reproduction by Colourscan, Singapore
Printed in China by Toppan Printing Co. (Shenzhen) Ltd.

Swimming goggles

Exercising with
weights

The clean
and jerk

Contents

What were the Olympics?

THE ORIGINS OF THE Olympic Games lie centuries ago in ancient Greece. The games were part of a religious festival. Greek life revolved around religion, and sports were a way for the people to honor their gods. There were many local festivals, but four national festivals called the Panhellenic Games were open to competitors from all Greek regions and colonies. These were the Pythian, the Nemean, the Isthmian, and the Olympic Games. They alternated so that there was a national athletic festival every year.

DELPHI STADIUM
Delphi was sacred to Apollo, and the Greeks thought that it stood at the center of the world. In the 5th century B.C., they built this 7,000-seat athletics stadium on the hillside above the great Temple of Apollo. The spectators' stand and seats for supervisors can be seen among the ruins today.

HONORING APOLLO
Different games were celebrations to honor different gods and were held at or near religious sanctuaries. The Pythian Games were held in Delphi in honor of Apollo. The Isthmian Games in Corinth honored Poseidon. Zeus was honored at the Nemean Games in Nemea and at the Olympic Games in Olympia.

Ancient Greek carving of Apollo (right)

This ancient Greek vessel shows athletes racing in armor

Laurel wreaths were awarded at the Pythian Games

Shield with runner's personal symbols on the outside

Fresh wild celery was awarded at the Nemean Games

Wreaths of olive leaves were awarded at the Olympic Games

Panathenaic amphora

RUNNER'S PRIZE
Winners at the Panathenaic Games in Athens were awarded an amphora, a two-handled vessel, full of the finest olive oil. It was decorated with scenes of their particular event. This amphora shows racing in armor. Athletics and war were closely linked. Competing in sports was a way of keeping fit for battle.

Athlete wearing a helmet and carrying a shield as he races

FLORAL TRIBUTES
At the Panhellenic Games, floral tributes were given to the winners. Most prized of all was an Olympic olive wreath, cut from a sacred tree that stood behind Zeus temple at Olympia. Originally the athletes were amateurs, but eventually, at all but the Olympic Games, they received prize money and were even paid for appearing.

Wreaths of pine branches were award at the Isthmian Game

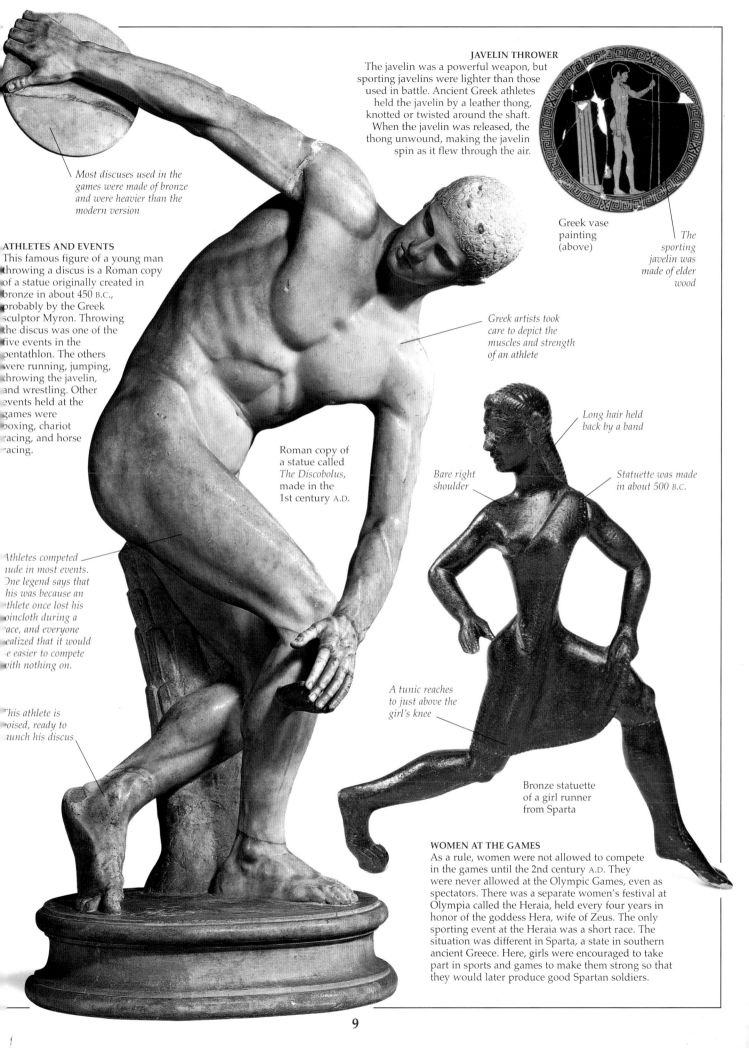

*Most discuses used in the
games were made of bronze
and were heavier than the
modern version*

JAVELIN THROWER

The javelin was a powerful weapon, but
sporting javelins were lighter than those
used in battle. Ancient Greek athletes
held the javelin by a leather thong,
knotted or twisted around the shaft.
When the javelin was released, the
thong unwound, making the javelin
spin as it flew through the air.

Greek vase
painting
(above)

*The
sporting
javelin was
made of elder
wood*

ATHLETES AND EVENTS

This famous figure of a young man
throwing a discus is a Roman copy
of a statue originally created in
bronze in about 450 B.C.,
probably by the Greek
sculptor Myron. Throwing
the discus was one of the
five events in the
pentathlon. The others
were running, jumping,
throwing the javelin,
and wrestling. Other
events held at the
games were
boxing, chariot
racing, and horse
racing.

*Greek artists took
care to depict the
muscles and strength
of an athlete*

Roman copy of
a statue called
The Discobolus,
made in the
1st century A.D.

*Long hair held
back by a band*

*Bare right
shoulder*

*Statuette was made
in about 500 B.C.*

*Athletes competed
nude in most events.
One legend says that
this was because an
athlete once lost his
loincloth during a
race, and everyone
realized that it would
be easier to compete
with nothing on.*

*A tunic reaches
to just above the
girl's knee*

*This athlete is
poised, ready to
launch his discus*

Bronze statuette
of a girl runner
from Sparta

WOMEN AT THE GAMES

As a rule, women were not allowed to compete
in the games until the 2nd century A.D. They
were never allowed at the Olympic Games, even as
spectators. There was a separate women's festival at
Olympia called the Heraia, held every four years in
honor of the goddess Hera, wife of Zeus. The only
sporting event at the Heraia was a short race. The
situation was different in Sparta, a state in southern
ancient Greece. Here, girls were encouraged to take
part in sports and games to make them strong so that
they would later produce good Spartan soldiers.

The ancient games

VICTORY
The winged figure on this cast of a stone seal represents Nike, or Victory. She is crowning an athlete with an olive wreath. Winning was everything at the Olympics. Losers were quickly forgotten.

THE FIRST RECORD of the Olympic Games dates from 776 B.C., but they were probably established hundreds of years before that. The Olympics began as a small event but gradually gained popularity to become the premier festival in Greece. For at least a thousand years, they were held every four years, and they survived in spite of numerous wars and the Roman invasion of Greece in about A.D. 150. The games became so important that the Greeks recorded events according to the Olympiad, the four-year period in which they took place.

The Olympic Games were held in honor of Zeus. On the third day of the games, a procession of competitors, judges, and important guests made its way to the Altar of Zeus, where 100 oxen were sacrificed. The most important building at Olympia was the great Temple of Zeus. Inside stood a statue of the god, cast in gold and ivory, and it was one of the seven wonders of the ancient world. At the end of the 4th century A.D., the statue was taken to a palace in Istanbul, where it was later destroyed in a fire.

Zeus is said to have hurled a thunderbolt and claimed the spot where it landed in Olympia as his sacred precinct

Zeus is usually depicted as strong, bearded, and middle-aged

Roman statuette of Zeus from 2nd century B.C.

MUSIC AND DANCE
The religious ceremonies and sporting events at Olympia were part of a greater festival. Tens of thousands of spectators flocked there to watch the games and visit the temples. They were kept well entertained by singers, dancers, magicians, public speakers, and poets. Food and flower sellers, peddlers, and bookmakers set up their tents and stalls outside the sacred site.

THE OLYMPIC TRUCE
Ancient Greece was not a single country but a collection of independent city-states that were often at war with each other. During the Olympic Games, an agreement called the Sacred Truce declared that all hostilities must cease for a month. The truce was backed by peace treaties, such as the one shown on this tablet between the state of Elis, containing Olympia, and a neighboring state.

Gymnasium, where runners and throwers trained

Palaistra, for jumping and combat training

The Temple of Hera, the first temple on the site

Treasuries, where valuables were stored

Stadium – 630 ft (192 m) long and 105 ft (32 m) wide

OLYMPIA

This remote religious sanctuary was about 31 miles (50 km) from the city of Elis. There was no town or city at Olympia. When the Olympics began in the 8th century B.C., the site consisted of a sacred area but no buildings. Over the next 1,000 years, many buildings were constructed, including temples, altars, colonnades, and sports arenas. This model of Olympia shows the site as it would have looked in about 100 B.C.

Probable site of the hippodrome, where chariot and horse racing took place

Open-air swimming pool with steps leading down from each side

Leonidaion, a hotel for visiting officials

Sacred olive tree

Temple of Zeus

Southern colonnade from which spectators could watch the chariots going to the hippodrome

Starting gates of the hippodrome

Heracles supporting the world on his shoulders for Atlas

The goddess Athena assisting Heracles

Section of a frieze from the Temple of Zeus at Olympia

HERACLES

According to myth, Olympia was created by the greatest Greek hero of them all, Heracles (or Hercules), son of Zeus. Heracles is famous for performing twelve seemingly impossible tasks, or labors. He started the Olympic Games in honor of Zeus to celebrate the completion of one of these tasks – the cleaning of the cattle stables of King Augeas of Elis.

THE PALAISTRA AT OLYMPIA

These columns are the remains of the palaistra at Olympia, where athletes trained for jumping and combat events. The palaistra was a low building around a central courtyard. It contained dressing rooms, baths, and a washroom. Every Greek city had its own palaistra.

Boxers wrapped leather thongs around their hands over a sheepskin lining

Boxing contests could last for several hours

OLYMPIC EVENTS

There were no team events at the ancient Olympics. To begin with, the only event was a short footrace – about 660 ft (200 m). Boxing and other sports were gradually added. Legend has it that Apollo beat Ares, the god of war, in the first boxing match at Olympia.

Boxing scene from an amphora given as a prize in about 336 B.C.

11

Olympia discovered

AFTER A.D. 261, THERE ARE no further records of Olympic winners, so we do not know for certain when the ancient games came to an end. When Rome made Greece part of its empire, the games began to decline. In A.D. 393, the Christian emperor Theodosius I decreed that all pagan centers be closed down, and Olympia was eventually abandoned. A succession of invaders destroyed the site, and any remaining buildings were ruined by earthquakes and fires. Flooding from nearby rivers finally covered the ruins with several feet of mud, and it was 1,000 years before Olympia's buildings were seen again.

END OF THE GAMES
A portrait of the Roman emperor Theodosius II appears on this ancient gold coin. In A.D. 426, Theodosius II had the Temple of Zeus and other buildings at Olympia burned down. This may have been when the Olympic Games finally came to an end.

ERNST CURTIUS
Archaeologists began the search for Olympia in the 18th century, but the most important excavations were carried out between 1875 and 1891 by the German Archaeological Institute. Directed by Professor Ernst Curtius, a team unearthed the remains of almost all the buildings. They found 130 statues and more than 6,000 clay, gold, and bronze objects.

Ernst Curtius in about 1880

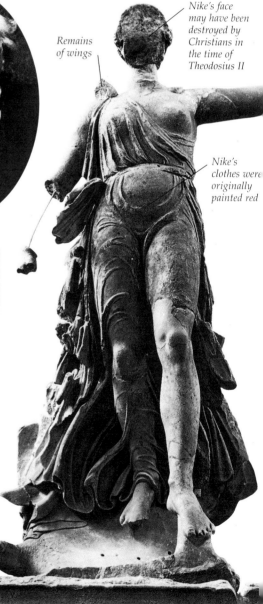

Nike's face may have been destroyed by Christians in the time of Theodosius II

Remains of wings

Nike's clothes were originally painted red

MODERN-DAY EXCAVATIONS
Most of Olympia had been explored by the end of the 19th century, but excavations have continued on a smaller scale up to the present day. For example, between 1958 and 1961, a German team finished excavating the stadium and rebuilt the banked spectator area.

RUINED GYMNASIUM
The German archaeologists did not find any buildings still standing at Olympia, but they reconstructed many of the toppled remains. This view shows part of the huge gymnasium complex, where athletes trained under cover. It was large enough to contain a running track the same length as the main stadium.

STATUE OF NIKE
This statue of Nike, or Victory, descending from the heavens remarkably survived almost in one piece. Made in 425 B.C. by Paionios of Mende, the statue is 9.8 ft (3 m) tall. It stood on top of a column, a further 29.5 ft (9 m) high, in front of the Temple of Zeus.

BRONZE GODDESS
Archaeologists have found hundreds of statuettes and figurines, mostly of bronze, like this goddess, or of terra-cotta. There are gods, heroes, warriors, runners, animals, and chariots complete with charioteers. The figures were offered to the gods by athletes and spectators.

Most statues at Olympia were paid for by winning athletes and dedicated to Zeus

Long nose-piece and cheek guards are typical of a Corinthian helmet

SPOILS OF WAR
Ancient Greek warriors gave arms and armor captured in battle as offerings to the gods. Shields, breastplates, helmets, arrowheads, spears, and other weapons have all been found at Olympia. The bronze helmet above carries an inscription, which says that it was dedicated to Zeus as spoil taken from the Corinthians.

Zeus carries off Ganymede

The boxer's face is covered in scars

This bronze head is 11 in (28 cm) high

Bronze statue of a goddess from 520 B.C.

CUTS AND BRUISES
This bronze head, found at Olympia in 1880, is a portrait of a boxer called Satyros. Boxing in ancient times was an even tougher sport than boxing today. There were no rounds to give the boxers a break, and no time limits. The sculptor gave this boxer wounds to make him look realistic.

ZEUS SEIZES GANYMEDE
Some finds at Olympia are amazingly well preserved. This terra-cotta statue of Zeus and Ganymede was found in the stadium area. It was made in 470 B.C., possibly by a famous sculptor called Phidias, who made many of the statues at Olympia in his workshop near the gymnasium. In Greek legend, Zeus carried off Ganymede to be his cupbearer because of Ganymede's beauty.

The Olympics reborn

MORE THAN 1,500 YEARS after the ancient Greek Olympic Games came to an end, the Frenchman Baron Pierre de Coubertin had a dream – to bring the games back to life. At a conference on international sports, held in Paris in 1894, Coubertin put forward a resolution to revive the games. His idea was enthusiastically received and the International Olympic Committee (IOC) was founded, with Coubertin among its members. Just two years later, in Athens in April 1896, the king of Greece declared open the first Olympic Games of the modern era. Over the next 100 years, the Olympics gradually grew into the fabulous sporting occasion we know today.

Carving of Zeus

BURIED HEART
At Olympia, the Greeks raised a monument to Pierre de Coubertin to thank him for his efforts in reviving the Olympics. Coubertin's last wish was that his heart should be kept forever at Olympia. It is buried beneath the monument.

Inscription honors Coubertin's work in reviving the Olympic Games

Coubertin won a gold medal for poetry at the Stockholm games in 1912

Founding father

Without Baron Pierre de Coubertin, it is unlikely that the modern Olympic Games would exist. Coubertin believed that sports were vital for the mental as well as the physical development of young people, and that international sporting competition would help people from different nations to become friends. Coubertin himself was a keen sportsman, though not an outstanding one.

MEMORIAL BADGE
This memorial medal was struck "to the reviver of the Olympic Games." Coubertin was fascinated by ancient Greece. His dream of a modern Olympics was boosted when archaeologists discovered the ruins of Olympia in 1875.

PIERRE DE COUBERTIN
Pierre de Coubertin was born in Paris, France, on New Year's Day 1863. He was president of the International Olympic Committee from 1896 to 1925 and was awarded the Nobel Peace Prize in 1920. He died in Geneva, Switzerland, in 1937.

BIRTH OF THE RINGS
On a visit to Delphi, site of the ancient Pythian Games, Pierre de Coubertin saw an emblem of five linked rings on this altar. It gave him the idea for the design on the Olympic flag. The five intertwined rings symbolized the five continents that participated in the games: Africa, Asia, America, Europe, and Australasia.

Wreath of olive leaves laid in remembrance

The five-ring symbol on this ancient Greek altar at Delphi represented five circles on a sacred discus, in which the terms of the truce for the Pythian Games were inscribed

THE FIRST STADIUM
The Panathenean Stadium in Athens was specially built for the 1896 Olympic Games. It was a marble replica of an ancient stadium originally built in 330 B.C., and it was built on the same site. The arena was long and narrow, and runners in the longer races had to slow down for the tight turns at each end of the track.

JUST THE TICKET
A ticket for the Olympic Games in 1896 cost two drachmas. More than 60,000 spectators turned up for the opening day. The competitors were not the world's best athletes, because anybody could take part. Most competitors were Greek; some were tourists who entered at the last minute.

POSTERS AND POSTAGE
The design for this poster (left) for the 1896 games has a classical feel, showing the ancient buildings of the Acropolis. The games had no official sponsors, though the Greek royal family offered some financial support. Special postage stamps and a lottery also helped to fund the games.

1896 winner's medal

Greek lettering denoting the Olympic Games

Image of the Acropolis in Athens

A winner's medal in 1896 was silver, not gold

MARATHON STARTS
One of the races in 1896 was run from the plains of Marathon, north of Athens, to the new stadium. It was run in honor of Pheidippides, a legendary warrior who, after the Battle of Marathon in 490 B.C., ran from the battlefield with news of the victory of the Athenians over the Persians. He then dropped dead. The 1896 marathon was appropriately won by a Greek runner, Spiridon Loues, seen here in national dress.

FIRST MEDALS WON
Coubertin thought that the awarding of medals would be an incentive to athletes to take part in the Olympics. Winners in Athens in 1896 were presented with a silver medal, an olive branch, and a certificate; runners-up received a copper medal and a sprig of laurel.

Traditions

ANCIENT TRADITIONS
The inside of a cup, showing a boxer at prayer. At the ancient Olympics, whole days were given over to religious ceremonies.

"IN THE NAME OF all the competitors, I promise that we shall take part in these Olympic Games, respecting and abiding by the rules which govern them, in the true spirit of sportsmanship, for the glory of sport, and the honor of our teams." So goes the Olympic oath, spoken by one athlete at every Olympic Games opening ceremony. It reminds us of the Olympic tradition that competition must be fair and friendly, and that taking part is more important than winning. All the Olympic ceremonies and symbols reflect the aim of the Olympic movement to promote understanding between the nations of the world.

Unusual openwork design

1,688 torches were used in the 1948 relay This is the torch used by the last runner at the opening ceremony

TORCH RELAY
As a symbol of international unity, the Olympic flame is taken by torch relay across national borders from the ancient site of Olympia to the Olympic venue. Where possible, it is taken by runners, who run 1,094 yd (1 km) each. Sometimes it goes by boat or plane. The flame is transferred from torch to torch. When it reaches the stadium, it is taken around the track and then used to ignite the main flame, which burns throughout the games.

1936 torch was modeled on those seen on ancient artifacts

1936 – Berlin, Germany. This was the first time the flame was lit at Olympia and taken by torch relay. It went via Athens and covered 1,910 miles (3,075 km).

Olympic rings and wreath

1948 – London, England. The torch relay was diverted to go past Coubertin's tomb.

Only 22 torches were made, so, for the first time, the runners did not each have their own torch

Fluted handle

LIGHTING THE FLAME
The Olympic flame is lit at the altar of the goddess Hera at Olympia, where a flame burned during the ancient Olympic Games. A torch is lit using a concave mirror to concentrate light from the sun. Before it begins the journey to the Olympic stadium, it is used to light a flame in the Coubertin Grove in honor of Pierre de Coubertin.

1952 – Helsinki, Finland. To the delight of the crowd, the great Finnish runners Paavo Nurmi and Hannes Kolehmainen carried the torch into the Olympic stadium.

Poster advertising the 1928 Olympic Games

Opening ceremony, Nagano, Japan, 1998

FIRST LIGHT
The Olympic flame was first lit at the 1928 Olympic Games in Amsterdam. It burned throughout the games at the top of a 164-ft- (50-m-) high tower in the stadium.

OPENING CEREMONY
A spectacular display now always forms part of the opening ceremony at the Olympic Games. After the display, the competitors enter the stadium. The Greek team always leads the parade, and the host team always enters last. One of the athletes and one of the judges take the Olympic oath of fair play on behalf of the others. At the closing ceremony, the president of the International Olympic Committee calls for the youth of the world to gather again in four years' time.

Gold-plated upper part

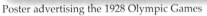

1952 – Oslo, Norway.
The torch relay for the Winter Games started at the historic Norwegian town of Morgedal.

1960 – Squaw Valley, United States. The main flame for these Winter Games was lit from this torch by the 1952 speed-skating champion Kenneth Henry.

1968 – Mexico City, Mexico. Enriqueta Basilio became the first woman to light the flame.

Silver-plated handle

1980 – Moscow, Soviet Union. Sergei Belov and Victor Saneyev were the last runners.

Leather handle with a metallic ring

1992 – Albertville, France. The flame was lit by the French soccer star Michel Platini and a local child.

Dove design on the poster for the Moscow games of 1980

DOVES OF PEACE
During the opening ceremony, hundreds of doves are released into the air from cages in the stadium as a symbol of peace. Doves of peace were released at the very first modern Olympic Games in 1896.

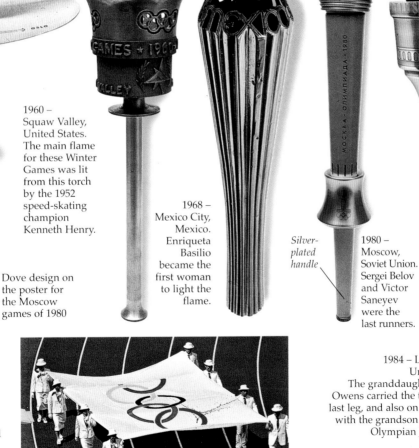

1984 – Los Angeles, United States. The granddaughter of Jesse Owens carried the torch on the last leg, and also on the first leg with the grandson of the great Olympian Jim Thorpe.

OLYMPIC FLAG
The Olympic flag has flown at the games since 1920. It was designed to include at least one color in the flag of every country. At the closing ceremony, the flag is given to a representative of the hosts of the next games.

From the beginning

THE OLYMPIC Games are held in the first year of each four-year Olympiad. Athens 1896 was in the I Olympiad; Sydney 2000 will be the games of the XXVII (27th) Olympiad. They will be in fact only the 24th Summer Olympic Games because the games of three Olympiads were not held, owing to war. The first Winter Olympic Games were held in 1924 in the VIII (8th) Olympiad. There was little interest in the Summer Games of 1900 and 1904, so a 10th-anniversary games were held in 1906 in Athens. These were known as the Interim or Intercalcated Games.

BRONZE MEDAL
This medal, struck to commemorate the first modern Olympic Games in Athens, shows the goddess Athena holding an olive wreath.

OLYMPIC SOUVENIR
Many different souvenirs have been made for the Olympic Games. This is a clothing pin commemorating the Paris games of 1900.

THE GREAT STADIUM
SHEPHERD'S BUSH LONDON

THE OLYMPIC GAMES 1908
PROGRAMME
6d

LONDON 1908
London had less than two years to prepare for the 1908 Olympics, but the games were still the best organized to that time.

Program cover for the 1908 games

1896	1900	1904	1908	1912	1920
ATHENS, GREECE All competitors at the first modern games were men. American students took the athletics by storm, although they did not arrive until the eve of the games because of a mix-up with dates. Among them was the first Olympic champion, the triple jumper James Connolly. The cricket and soccer events were canceled owing to lack of entrants.	**PARIS, FRANCE** Held as part of the Paris International Exhibition, the games became a sideshow to the main event. They were spread over five months and there was little interest from the public. The facilities were substandard and the swimming was held in the river Seine. The American Ray Ewry won three jumping events, to start his career haul of ten golds.	**ST. LOUIS, UNITED STATES** As in Paris, the St. Louis games were part of a trade fair. Some non-Olympic sports were included for boys. There were fewer athletes than in 1900 because of the difficulty of traveling from Europe. Only one athletics event was won by a non-American – the Irishman Thomas Kiely won the decathlon.	**LONDON, ENGLAND** The games should have been held in Rome, but the Italian government had to divert funds to help the victims of the eruption of Mount Vesuvius in 1906. The lasting image is of the marathon runner Dorando Pietri being helped over the line to first place. He was disqualified but was later given a special gold cup by Queen Alexandra.	**STOCKHOLM, SWEDEN** The 1912 games were the most efficient so far. Among the new events were women's swimming and the modern pentathlon, devised by Pierre de Coubertin as a test of the all-around sportsman. Hannes Kolehmainen, the first of the "flying Finns," took gold in the 5,000 m, 10,000 m, and cross-country.	**ANTWERP, BELGIUM** The first games after World War I saw the Olympic flag flying for the first time. The Olympic oath was also heard for the first time. Germany, Bulgaria, Hungary, and Turkey were not invited because of their part in starting the war. On the track, the Finnish distance runner Paavo Nurmi made his mark.

18

PARIS - LYON - MÉDITERRANÉE

AUX VAINQUEURS DU CONCOURS DE LA VIII.me OLYMPIADE
CHAMONIX.MONT-BLANC
25 Janvier-5 Février 1924

OLYMPIC GAMES
3ᴰ
1948

The Olympic rings are part of the stamp design

THREEPENNY STAMP
The British Post Office issued a special set of stamps to commemorate the 1948 London Olympics.

Insignia of the SS

SS INSIGNIA
The German chancellor Adolf Hitler used the Berlin Olympics as a propaganda exercise for the Third Reich rather than a celebration of sports. More Nazi flags flew at the venues than Olympic flags.

Badge of the SS, the Nazi military police

Eagle emblem, as used in the Roman Empire

TOP VAULTER
The American pole-vaulter Bob Richards won the gold at the Helsinki games. He went on to repeat his success four years later in Melbourne, Australia.

CHAMONIX POSTER
The Winter Olympic Games at Chamonix in 1924 were originally called International Winter Sports Week. They were not officially recognized as the Olympics until 1926.

MASCOT

U.S. MASCOT
Smoky was adopted as the mascot for the 1932 Summer Games. He was born in the Olympic Village just before the games.

Nazi badge

The swastika was the symbol of the Nazi party

1924	1928	1932	1936	1948	1952
CHAMONIX, FRANCE The games at Chamonix were the first separate Winter Olympics. The first gold medalist was the American speed skater Charles Jewtraw. He won the 500 m on January 26. **PARIS, FRANCE** This was a far better event than that of 1900. Stars included Paavo Nurmi and Johnny Weissmuller in the swimming pool.	**ST. MORITZ, SWITZERLAND** Sonja Henie, aged only 15, was the star of the Winter Games, winning her first figure skating title. **AMSTERDAM, NETHERLANDS** For the first time, women could enter some of the athletics events. Germany was invited for the first time since World War I.	**LAKE PLACID, UNITED STATES** Snow was brought over by trucks from Canada for some events. Figure skating was held indoors for the first time. **LOS ANGELES, UNITED STATES** The Great Depression did not stop the games, but it did stop many athletes from going. Mildred ("Babe") Didrikson won the 80 m hurdles and javelin.	**GARMISCH-PARTENKIRCHEN, GERMANY** At great expense, many new facilities were built in the southern German resort of Garmisch. Alpine skiing events took place for the first time. **BERLIN, GERMANY** These games are best remembered for the American sprinter Jesse Owens.	**ST. MORITZ, SWITZERLAND** The first games after World War II were given to Switzerland, largely because it had stayed neutral. St. Moritz still had its 1928 facilities. **LONDON, ENGLAND** The 1948 Summer Games were centered on the Empire Stadium, Wembley. They helped to bring many countries back together after the war.	**OSLO, NORWAY** Norwegian winter sports fans attended the games in great numbers. There were an estimated 150,000 at the ski jumping. **HELSINKI, FINLAND** The small Finnish city hosted the most successful games so far. There were nearly 7,000 athletes from 61 nations. On the track, Emil Zatopek won three gold medals.

Continued on next page

1956–2004

The second half of the 20th century saw changes in the Olympics. From the 1960s, television coverage turned them into a global event. This attracted commercial sponsors, who now help to pay for the games in return for the advertising they receive. A previous ban on professionals has been lifted, although most competitors are still amateurs. The Winter Games have moved to a new four-year cycle, two years out of step with the Summer Games.

Karl Schranz lo out in 1968 too. He was allowed a rerun after a person crossed his path. He the had the fastest time, but was later disqualifie for missing two gates before he was distracted in his first run

PRO OUT
The Austrian skier Karl Schranz was banned on the day before the Sapporo games began for accepting sponsorship money, and therefore not being a true amateur. Thirty-nine other athletes were in the same position, but Schranz was the only one banned.

BOYCOTTS
After a New Zealand rugby tour of apartheid-governed South Africa, 24 teams boycotted the Montre games. They objected to New Zealand's being there.

CORTINA 1956
Commercial sponsors helped this northern Italian town to build new venues for the Winter Games. There were Soviet competitors for the first time since 1908.

Design for the 1956 Winter Olympics

FOSBURY FLOP
In 1968, Dick Fosbury won high-jump gold for the United States by clearing the bar shoulders first rather than by straddling it. This new style was adopted by most high jumpers and became known as the Fosbury flop.

1956	1960	1964	1968	1972	1976
CORTINA, ITALY The Soviet Union dominated the ice hockey. The Austrian Anton Sailer won all three Alpine titles. **MELBOURNE, AUSTRALIA** The Summer Games were the first held outside Europe or America. Quarantine rules prevented horses from entering the country, so the equestrian events were held in Sweden.	**SQUAW VALLEY, UNITED STATES** A resort was built for the games. Walt Disney devised the opening ceremony. **ROME, ITALY** The games were broadcast live on European TV. Cassius Clay (Muhammad Ali) won gold in the boxing. Abebe Bikila won the marathon barefoot. The first Paralympics took place afterward.	**INNSBRUCK, AUSTRIA** Poor weather in this resort meant that thousands of tons of snow had to be taken to the ski runs. **TOKYO, JAPAN** The Japanese spared no expense, building a new road system around Tokyo. The flame was lit by a student who was born near Hiroshima in 1945 on the day the atomic bomb fell.	**GRENOBLE, FRANCE** Venues for the Winter Games were spread around the region. The Frenchman Jean-Claude Killy won all the Alpine events. **MEXICO CITY, MEXICO** The high altitude meant that distance runners struggled to breathe in the thin air. It helped Bob Beamon to a long-jump world record, which lasted until 1991.	**SAPPORO, JAPAN** The huge sums given by TV companies for rights to the Winter Games paid for the fabulous facilities in this Japanese city. **MUNICH, GERMANY** Seventeen people died in a terrorist attack on the Israeli team. In the games, the U.S. swimmer Mark Spitz won seven golds and the Soviet gymnast Olga Korbut won three.	**INNSBRUCK, AUSTRIA** The games were moved from Denver because of spiraling costs. The German skier Rosi Mittermaier won two golds and a silver. **MONTREAL, CANAD/** There was extra security at the games because of the events of 1972. On the track, Lasse Viren repeated the 5,000 m and 10,000 m double.

A "human torch" was part of the elaborate display in Moscow

1980 OPENING
More than 100,000 spectators watched the opening ceremony in the Lenin Stadium in Moscow. Some teams protested against the Soviets by marching under the Olympic flag rather than their countries' flags.

Costume reflects the American flag

Sydney 2000 ™©

The eagle is an emblem of the United States

SAM THE EAGLE
The mascot for the 1984 Los Angeles games was the stars-and-stripes-clad Sam the Eagle.

DRUG SHAME
At Seoul, in the Olympics' worst drug scandal, the Canadian Ben Johnson failed a drug test. He was stripped of his medal three days after winning the 100 m in world-record time.

SYDNEY LOGO
In 1993, Australia's largest city, Sydney, was awarded the 2000 Olympic Games, dubbed the Millennium Games. More than 10,000 competitors and more than 1 million visitors are expected to attend.

1980	1984	1988	1992/1994	1996/1998	2000 and beyond
LAKE PLACID, UNITED STATES Artificial snow made its Winter Olympics debut. American Eric Heiden won five speed-skating golds. **MOSCOW, SOVIET UNION** Many countries boycotted the games because of the Soviet invasion of Afghanistan. British rivals Coe and Ovett won one gold medal each in the athletics.	**SARAJEVO, YUGOSLAVIA** Stars of the Winter Games were British ice dancers Torvill and Dean. Winter Paralympics were held for the first time. **LOS ANGELES, UNITED STATES** The 1932 stadium was used again. There was a Soviet boycott, but the games are better remembered for the performance of the American Carl Lewis.	**CALGARY, CANADA** The most successful competitor was the Finnish ski-jumper Matti Nykaenen, who won three golds. **SEOUL, KOREA** There were no major boycotts, and athletes from 159 countries took part. On the track, Florence Griffith-Joyner won three sprint medals. Kristin Otto of East Germany swam to six golds.	**ALBERTVILLE, FRANCE** New sports in the Winter Games included freestyle skiing. **BARCELONA, SPAIN** Athletes of the old Soviet Union entered as the Unified Team. South Africa returned, plus a reunited Germany. **LILLEHAMMER, NORWAY** In 1994, the new four-year cycle of Winter Games began.	**ATLANTA, UNITED STATES** In 1996, Atlanta held the Centenary Games. Not even a bomb in the Centennial Olympic Park could spoil the party. Michael Johnson completed the first-ever 200 m and 400 m double. **NAGANO, JAPAN** Curling, women's ice hockey, and snowboarding made their debut.	**SYDNEY, AUSTRALIA** New Olympic sports in Sydney will be tae kwon do and the triathlon. **SALT LAKE CITY, UNITED STATES** The 2002 Winter Olympics have been awarded to Salt Lake City, on the eastern side of the Rockies. **ATHENS, GREECE** In 2004, the Olympics will be in Athens, site of the 1896 games.

The Summer Games

COMPETITORS AT THE SYDNEY Olympic Games in 2000 will take part in a total of 28 different sports and groups of sports. Within these sports are nearly 300 individual and team events at which medals will be won. Some team events, such as the athletic relays, are separate from the individual events; others, such as the equestrian sport of show jumping, are decided by combining the results of a country's individual representatives. Two Olympic events are made up of a combination of different sports. They are the modern pentathlon, consisting of épée fencing, swimming, pistol shooting, running, and riding; and the triathlon, consisting of running, swimming, and cycling. The triathlon will be included at the Olympic Games for the first time in Sydney.

HURDLING
There are two sprint hurdling events – 100 m for women and 110 m for men (shown here is the British athlete Colin Jackson) over 10 hurdles, and the 400 m, over 10 slightly lower hurdles. Men also run the 3,000 m steeplechase, over 28 hurdles and 7 water jumps.

Athletics

Most of the events in track and field athletics fall into three categories – running events, throwing events, and jumping events. Other events are walking and the combined events of the 10-discipline decathlon for men and the 7-discipline heptathlon for women.

Men's javelins are 8.8 ft (2.7 m) long; women's are 7.5 ft (2.3 m) long

Sprinters use starting blocks

JAVELIN
The javelin is one of the four Olympic throwing events. This drawing shows the 1908 and 1912 gold medalist Erik Lemming of Sweden. The other throwing events are the shot put, discus, and hammer. In each event, the competitor who throws the furthest wins gold.

Footplates can be adjusted to suit the athlete

RUNNING
Running events without hurdles can be divided into sprints (100, 200, and 400 m), middle-distance (800 and 1,500 m), and long-distance (5,000 and 10,000 m and the marathon). Teams of four compete in relays at 4 x 100 m and 4 x 400 m, traditionally the last event of the track and field program.

JUMPING
The jumping events are long jump (shown here is Jackie Joyner-Kersee of the U.S.A.), high jump, triple jump, and pole vault. Long-jump and triple-jump athletes have six attempts. In the high jump and pole vault, the bar is raised, bit by bit, until one person is left.

Ribbon flows through the air, following the gymnast's arm movements

A short stick is attached to the ribbon

WATER SPORTS
Canoeing (shown here are the Germans Berro and Trummer in the 1992 Olympic C2 final), kayaking, sailing, and rowing are the Olympic water sports. In canoeing (with single-blade paddles) and kayaking (with double-blade paddles), there are flat-water sprints and white-water slaloms.

La Seu d'Urgell
406

Balletic movements are part of rhythmic gymnastics

The ribbon must be kept moving

TARGET SPORTS
Archery, as shown here, and shooting are the Olympic target sports. Archers shoot over four distances and combine the score. There are 15 shooting events in which competitors fire at stationary targets with rifles and pistols or at clay pigeons with shotguns.

Rhythmic gymnasts perform to music while using hand apparatus

GYMNASTICS
Artistic gymnastics consists of six disciplines for men (floor, pommel horse, rings, vault, parallel bars, and horizontal bar), and four disciplines for women (vault, uneven bars, balance beam, and floor). The separate events of trampolining and the ballet-like rhythmic gymnastics for women are also part of the gymnastic program.

Items of rhythmic gymnastic apparatus

The Spanish road cyclist Miguel Indurain at the 1996 Olympics

Clubs

Rope

Rhythmic gymnasts perform on the floor only

Hoops

CYCLING
Olympic cycling is divided into track cycling on an oval, banked track, road racing, and mountain biking. Track and road events include ordinary races, time trials against the clock, and pursuits, in which one cyclist or team attempts to catch another.

Continued on next page

Continued from previous page

*Weights are color-coded:
red = 55 lb (25 kg)
yellow = 33 lb (15 kg)*

*Weights are made
of rubber with
metal plates inside*

*Dressage riders
dress formally for
competition*

*Lifters are
divided into 10
weight classes*

EQUESTRIAN SPORTS

Riding has been part of the modern games since 1912. There are three events – show jumping, dressage, and the three-day event. The last of these is made up of dressage, cross-country, and show-jumping sections, held on separate days. In each event, there are individual and team golds to be won.

WEIGHT LIFTING

There are two weight lifting events in the Olympic Games. In the clean and jerk, the bar is lifted in two movements, first to the shoulders and then above the head. In the snatch, the bar is lifted above the head in one movement.

*The horse must
show obedience,
flexibility, and
athletic power*

*In halt, the
horse stands
still and
square*

COMBAT SPORTS

Olympic combat sports are judo (shown here are Kenzo Nakamura and Martin Schmidt in 1996), tae kwon do, boxing, wrestling, and fencing. There are three types of fencing – foil, épée, and saber. In the other sports, athletes are divided into weight categories. There are two wrestling styles – Greco-Roman and freestyle.

*In Olympic dressage,
the horse is asked to
perform only natural
movements*

RACKET AND BAT SPORTS
Tennis, table tennis, and badminton have all been added to the Olympic program since 1988. In each event, men and women can win medals for singles and doubles. Only badminton has a mixed-doubles event. Tennis is one of the few Olympic sports in which world-famous professionals are seen in action.

Most tennis rackets are strung with synthetic strings

AQUATICS
Swimming (shown here is the Australian Shane Gould in 1972), diving, synchronized swimming, and water polo take place in the 164-ft (50-m) pool. There are 16 events in both the men's and the women's swimming programs, including relays. Diving is divided into 3 m springboard and 10 m platform events.

Tennis was not included at the Olympics for many years because of the amateurs-only rule

Team sports
The Olympic team sports are basketball, soccer, volleyball, hockey (properly called field hockey), handball, baseball (for men only), and softball (for women only). Water polo is a team sport played in the pool. Many famous professionals compete in the team sports at the Olympics, now that restrictions on professional athletes have been lifted.

The 1992 "dream team" won each of their games by an average of 44 points

Basketball signed by the 1992 U.S. "dream team"

BASKETBALL
There are men's and women's basketball events. Olympic basketball includes one of the closest games in history. In the 1972 final, the U.S.S.R. broke the U.S.A.'s six-time gold-winning streak with a 51-50 win. Professionals were allowed into the 1992 games, won by the U.S.A.'s "dream team" – which was made up of multimillion-dollar players.

SOCCER
Olympic soccer is not as important as the World Cup, and many nations do not compete. All but three players in a men's team must be under 23, but there are no age restrictions for the women's event. This action is from the 1996 women's semifinal between Brazil and China.

VOLLEYBALL
Standard volleyball is played indoors with teams of six on each side of a high net. Players have to return the ball over the net with their hands. This picture shows the Netherlands versus Italy in 1996. Beach volleyball, with two players per side, was introduced to the Olympics at Atlanta 1996.

HOCKEY
Field hockey is a team game in which the ball is passed and shot with a stick by two eleven-person teams. Goals are scored in a way similar to soccer. No contact between players is allowed. Olympic hockey tournaments are played on an artificial surface. The women's match shown here is Australia versus Spain in 1996.

The Winter Games

ALL SPORTS AT THE Winter Olympic Games take place on ice or snow. Competitors at Salt Lake City in 2002 will take part in eight sports and groups of sports. Within these sports are more than 60 individual and team events in which medals will be won. As in the summer games, there are some team events in which the competitors compete individually and combine their scores. In other team events, such as curling, they compete together as a team. Curling is similar to bowling. It is played on an ice rink by two teams of four players who slide large stones across the ice toward a target.

Hungarian stamp commemorating Lake Placid 1980

NORDIC SKIING
Cross-country skiing and ski jumping (shown here is Didier Mollard of France), make up the sport of Nordic skiing. The skiing events, over distances from 5 to 50 km, are divided into classical events and freestyle events, in which a skating action is not allowed.

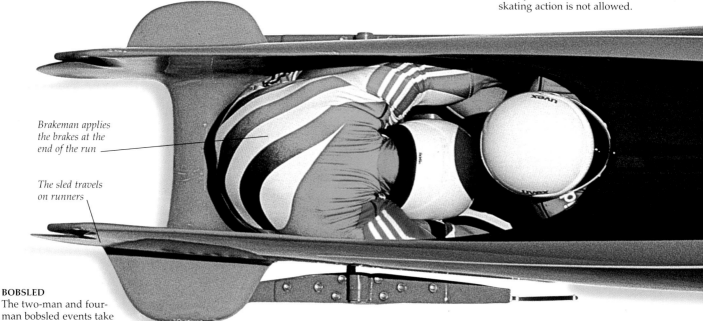

Brakeman applies the brakes at the end of the run

The sled travels on runners

BOBSLED
The two-man and four-man bobsled events take place on a steep, narrow, ice-covered run consisting of straights and bends. The riders push-start the sled at the top of the run, then jump in as it starts to gather speed. The driver, sitting at the front, steers the sled down the run. The team with the lowest total time over four runs wins. The Swiss two-man team of Gustav Weder and Donat Acklin are shown here winning gold in Lillehammer in 1994.

Rider lies flat on the luge to reduce air resistance

ICE HOCKEY
Fast and action-packed, ice hockey is the only field-type team sport in the Winter Olympics program. There are tournaments for both men and women. Six players, including a goalkeeper, from a team of 20 are allowed on the ice at any one time. This action is from a match between Finland and Russia in 1994.

LUGE
Tyler Seitz of Canada is seen here in the men's single luge event in 1998. A luge is a lightweight sled resembling a toboggan. Lugers ride down the same ice-covered run as the bobsledders. They travel feet first, steering around the bends with small foot and body movements. Luge events are men's and women's singles, and men's doubles. The riders with the lowest total time over a series of runs win.

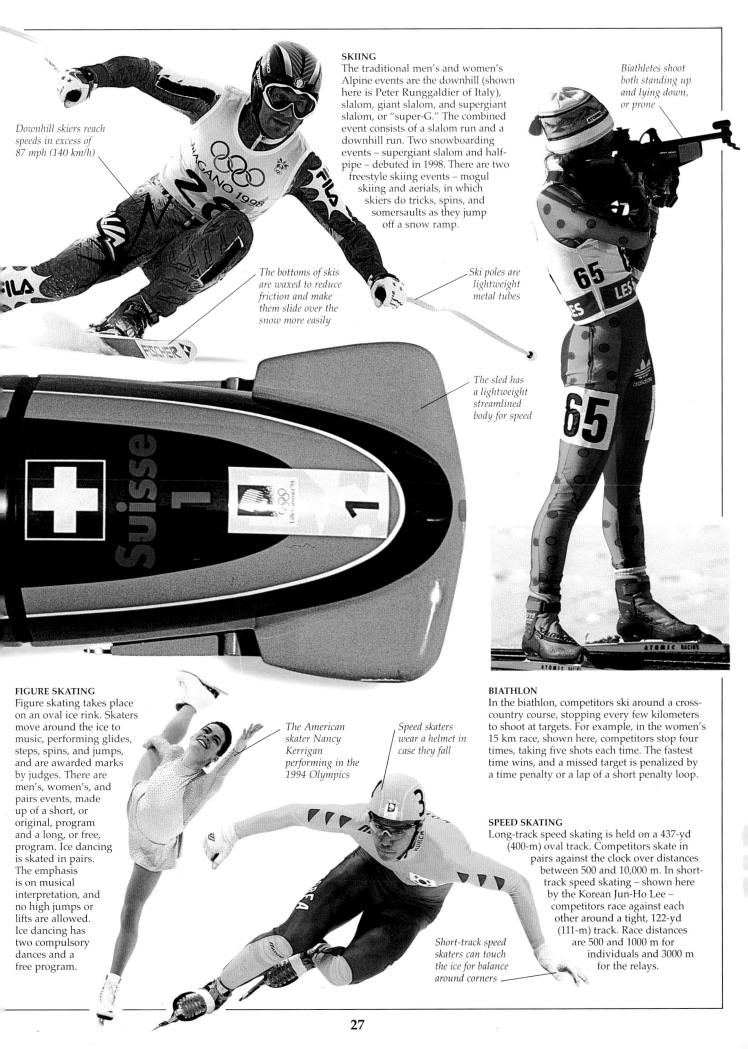

SKIING

The traditional men's and women's Alpine events are the downhill (shown here is Peter Runggaldier of Italy), slalom, giant slalom, and supergiant slalom, or "super-G." The combined event consists of a slalom run and a downhill run. Two snowboarding events – supergiant slalom and half-pipe – debuted in 1998. There are two freestyle skiing events – mogul skiing and aerials, in which skiers do tricks, spins, and somersaults as they jump off a snow ramp.

Downhill skiers reach speeds in excess of 87 mph (140 km/h)

The bottoms of skis are waxed to reduce friction and make them slide over the snow more easily

Ski poles are lightweight metal tubes

Biathletes shoot both standing up and lying down, or prone

The sled has a lightweight streamlined body for speed

FIGURE SKATING

Figure skating takes place on an oval ice rink. Skaters move around the ice to music, performing glides, steps, spins, and jumps, and are awarded marks by judges. There are men's, women's, and pairs events, made up of a short, or original, program and a long, or free, program. Ice dancing is skated in pairs. The emphasis is on musical interpretation, and no high jumps or lifts are allowed. Ice dancing has two compulsory dances and a free program.

The American skater Nancy Kerrigan performing in the 1994 Olympics

Speed skaters wear a helmet in case they fall

Short-track speed skaters can touch the ice for balance around corners

BIATHLON

In the biathlon, competitors ski around a cross-country course, stopping every few kilometers to shoot at targets. For example, in the women's 15 km race, shown here, competitors stop four times, taking five shots each time. The fastest time wins, and a missed target is penalized by a time penalty or a lap of a short penalty loop.

SPEED SKATING

Long-track speed skating is held on a 437-yd (400-m) oval track. Competitors skate in pairs against the clock over distances between 500 and 10,000 m. In short-track speed skating – shown here by the Korean Jun-Ho Lee – competitors race against each other around a tight, 122-yd (111-m) track. Race distances are 500 and 1000 m for individuals and 3000 m for the relays.

The Paralympics

THE SUMMER AND WINTER Paralympic Games are the foremost sports meetings for athletes with physical and mental disabilities. They are held in the same year and in the same host city as the Summer and Winter Olympics. The "Para" in Paralympics signifies that these games run beside the Olympics, complementing them. Athletes compete in one of several categories, depending on their particular disability. Currently, there are 18 sports in the Summer Games and 4 in the Winter Games.

A helmet similar to a cycling helmet is worn in case of a crash at high speed

SILVER MEDAL
This medal from the 1992 Barcelona Paralympics has lettering in Braille to allow blind people to read it.

Women marathon athletes reach speeds of more than 35 mph (60 km/h)

Athlete needs strong arms and upper body

Legs tucked underneath the body

The British marathon racer Rose Hill

Wheel with which the athlete pushes the chair forward

WHEELCHAIR RACES
Paralympians race in wheelchairs over all the standard distances from the 100 m to the marathon. Racing wheelchairs are as specialized as racing bicycles. Athletes steer by the front wheel, and for track races the steering can be adjusted so that a simple flick of a lever steers the chair around bends.

FENCING

Paralympic fencers, shown here competing at Barcelona in 1992, compete in three disciplines: foil, épée, and saber. Fencers sit in wheelchairs that are bolted to the floor to prevent them from tipping over. They attack by leaning forward and defend by leaning back.

LONG JUMP

There are jumping events in several disability categories. Shown here is Ricardo Ignacia of Brazil, competing in the long jump for amputees. He is wearing a specialized artificial limb, or prosthesis, that can stand the pounding of the run-up, takeoff, and landing.

BASKETBALL

Wheelchair basketball is one of the original Paralympic events. Most of the rules, such as team size, court size, and basket height, are those set down by the International Basketball Federation. The wheelchairs are designed to allow the players to accelerate and spin quickly. Intellectual-disability basketball will be played for the first time at the Paralympics at Sydney in 2000.

Bar attached to the front wheel for steering

Chair frame is 4.5 ft (1.4 m) long

SPRINTING

This is the British athlete Stuart Bryce competing in the 1992 Paralympics. His right leg is amputated above the knee. His prosthesis, complete with standard running shoe, allows him to complete sprint races only about 10 percent more slowly than Olympic champions.

Wheelchair racers wear three layers of gloves to prevent blisters

CYCLING

Road cycling became a Paralympic sport in 1988 and was followed by track cycling in 1996. Athletes compete in three categories – visually impaired, cerebral palsy, and amputees. Blind cyclists compete in road and track races on tandem cycles with a sighted partner. Here, the Americans Cara Dunney and Scott Evans compete in the 1996 tandem pursuit.

Comings and goings

Both the Summer and the Winter Games have a set program. The number of sports and events has gradually increased since the first modern games in 1896. It took a long time for the program to become settled. Many sports, including peculiar events such as underwater swimming and rope climbing, were dropped along the way, often after just a brief appearance. Some sports, such as archery and tennis, have been introduced, dropped, and reintroduced years later. Most sports now have men's and women's events, but up until the Second World War only a handful were included, and there were no women's events at all in 1896.

TENNIS
The first modern games featured tennis, which remained an Olympic sport until 1924. It was then dropped because the IOC and the International Tennis Federation disagreed over the definition of amateurism. It was re-introduced in 1988, and Steffi Graf and Miloslav Mecir won the singles.

A long jumper with weights, from an ancient Greek vase

JUMPING WITH WEIGHTS
The only jumping event at Olympia was the long jump with weights, which was part of the pentathlon. The athlete probably took a short run before swinging the weights forward to gain momentum for his jump. It may have been a single, double, or triple jump.

THE PANKRATION
Just about any tactics were allowed in the combat event called the pankration, a mixture of wrestling and boxing with no rounds or time limit. Only eye gouging and biting were against the rules, but pankratiasts often got away with both. The idea was to make the opponent submit.

Ancient games

For at least 50 years, until 728 B.C., a short sprint the length of the stadium at Olympia was the only event at the ancient games. Over the next 500 years, events were gradually added, including more footraces, wrestling, the pentathlon, boxing, horse racing, and chariot racing.

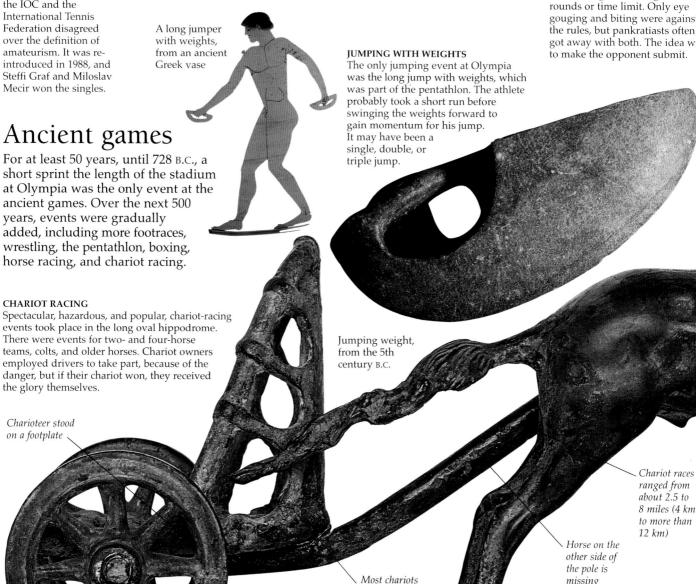

Jumping weight, from the 5th century B.C.

CHARIOT RACING
Spectacular, hazardous, and popular, chariot-racing events took place in the long oval hippodrome. There were events for two- and four-horse teams, colts, and older horses. Chariot owners employed drivers to take part, because of the danger, but if their chariot won, they received the glory themselves.

Charioteer stood on a footplate

Roman bronze model of a two-horse chariot

Most chariots were made of wood, wickerwork, and leather

Chariot races ranged from about 2.5 to 8 miles (4 km to more than 12 km)

Horse on the other side of the pole is missing

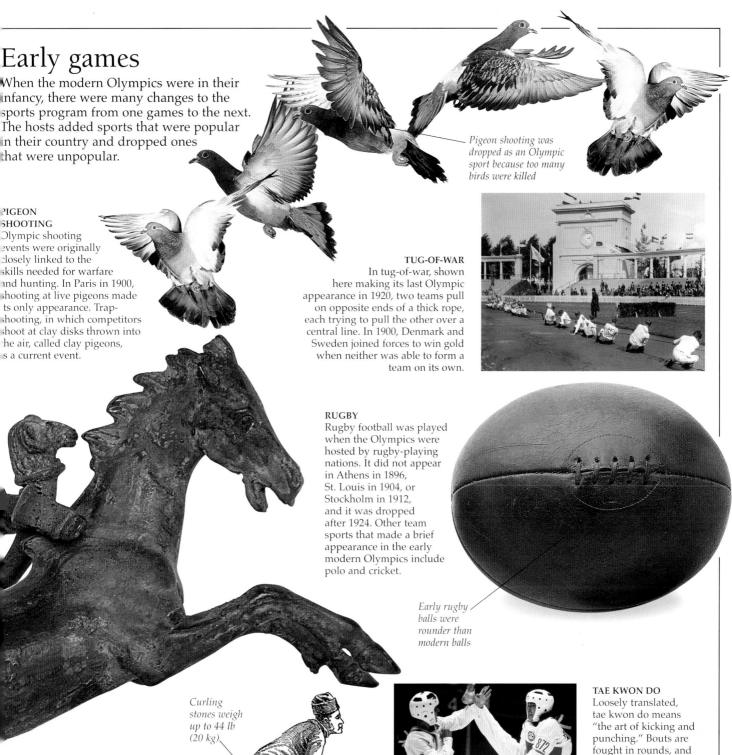

Early games

When the modern Olympics were in their infancy, there were many changes to the sports program from one games to the next. The hosts added sports that were popular in their country and dropped ones that were unpopular.

Pigeon shooting was dropped as an Olympic sport because too many birds were killed

PIGEON SHOOTING
Olympic shooting events were originally closely linked to the skills needed for warfare and hunting. In Paris in 1900, shooting at live pigeons made its only appearance. Trap-shooting, in which competitors shoot at clay disks thrown into the air, called clay pigeons, is a current event.

TUG-OF-WAR
In tug-of-war, shown here making its last Olympic appearance in 1920, two teams pull on opposite ends of a thick rope, each trying to pull the other over a central line. In 1900, Denmark and Sweden joined forces to win gold when neither was able to form a team on its own.

RUGBY
Rugby football was played when the Olympics were hosted by rugby-playing nations. It did not appear in Athens in 1896, St. Louis in 1904, or Stockholm in 1912, and it was dropped after 1924. Other team sports that made a brief appearance in the early modern Olympics include polo and cricket.

Early rugby balls were rounder than modern balls

Recent games

The Olympic program continues to expand. Events added recently include traditional sports, such as tennis, and newly established sports, such as snowboarding. International governing bodies make representations to the IOC for their sport to be included. To be part of the Summer Games, a sport must be played in 75 countries from four continents for men, and in 40 countries from three continents for women.

Curling stones weigh up to 44 lb (20 kg)

CURLING
The centuries-old game of curling was introduced to the Winter Olympics at Nagano in 1998. In curling, players slide a polished stone along the ice, trying to make it stop in the center of a target. The sport probably originated in Scotland but is most popular in Canada.

TAE KWON DO
Loosely translated, tae kwon do means "the art of kicking and punching." Bouts are fought in rounds, and points are scored by striking the opponent's trunk and face. The sport originated in Korea and will make its debut as an Olympic medal sport in 2000.

SYNCHRONIZED SWIMMING
As shown here by the Italian team in 1996, synchronized swimmers move in the water in time to music and in time with each other. "Synchro" was demonstrated in 1952, but it became a medal sport only in 1984.

Great Olympians

THE HISTORY OF THE OLYMPICS is full of inspirational and heroic performances, but what makes an athlete a great Olympian rather than just a great athlete? It might be winning at two or more Olympics in succession, or winning several events at the same games. Or perhaps it is simply taking part again and again, or upholding the Olympic ideal of sportsmanship despite losing. Of course, there are many great sportsmen and women who have never won Olympic gold, perhaps because of an injury or lack of form at the critical time, or because they were professional in the amateur era, or because their sports were not included in the Olympic program.

WINNER'S TABLET
This stone records the feats of a Roman athlete, Lucius, who competed "in all the athletic festivals in a manner worthy of victory."

JIM THORPE
Gold medals in both the decathlon and the track-and-field pentathlon (no longer an Olympic event), at Stockholm in 1912, established American Jim Thorpe as the greatest all-around athlete of the time. He went on to play major-league baseball and football.

Summer Olympians

Every Summer Olympics is remembered for one or more great performances on a track, in the pool, or in the gymnastics hall. Most prominence is given to athletes who win classic events, such as the 100 m or the marathon. Winners in the less well known sports, such as shooting and yachting, are often the unsung heroes of the games.

JESSE OWENS
The name of Jesse Owens, seen above in a still from Leni Riefenstahl's film *Olympia*, will always be associated with the Berlin Olympics of 1936. Under the gaze of the racists of the Nazi regime, Owens won gold in the 100 m, 200 m, long jump, and 4 x 100 m relay, setting two Olympic records and a world record.

EMIL ZATOPEK
At the 1952 games in Helsinki, Czechoslovakian army officer and distance runner Emil Zatopek, seen here leading a heat of the 5,000 m, became the only athlete in Olympic history to win gold in the 5,000 m, 10,000 m, and marathon at the same games.

Simple heel outline

Thin leather sole with spikes

Soft leather upper

Emil Zatopek's running shoe

PAAVO NURMI

Finnish middle-distance runner Paavo Nurmi, seen here on the shoulder of his great rival Willie Ritola, was one of the first runners to take a scientific approach to his training. It helped him to win a total of twelve Olympic medals, nine of them gold, at the 1920, 1924, and 1928 Olympics. In 1924, he won the 1,500 m and recovered in time to win the 5,000 m less than an hour later.

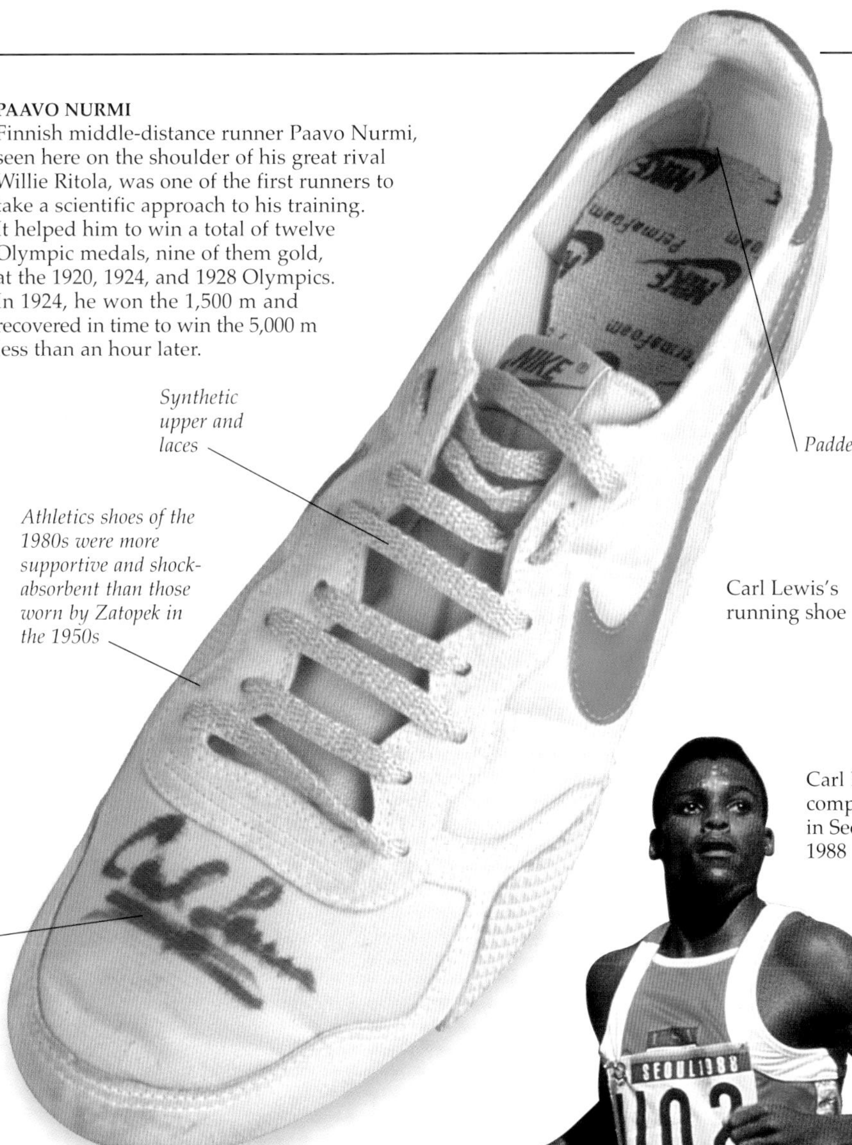

Synthetic upper and laces

Padded heel

Athletics shoes of the 1980s were more supportive and shock-absorbent than those worn by Zatopek in the 1950s

Carl Lewis's running shoe

Carl Lewis's signature

Carl Lewis competing in Seoul in 1988

Tanni Grey competed at several different distances

CARL LEWIS

The American sprinter and long jumper Carl Lewis was at the top of his form throughout the 1980s. His greatest Olympic year was 1984, when he won the 100 m, the 200 m, the long jump, and the sprint relay, matching the feat of Jesse Owens in 1936. He retained his 100 m and long-jump titles in 1988 and won another relay gold in 1992.

TANNI GREY

The British wheelchair athlete Tanni Grey, seen here winning gold in the 400 m at Barcelona in 1992, is one of the great Paralympians. She won her first medal, a bronze, in Seoul in 1988, added four golds in Barcelona, and just missed out on a medal in Atlanta in 1996.

NADIA COMANECI

Having started gymnastic training aged just 6, the Romanian gymnast Nadia Comaneci developed a perfect sense of timing and balance. At age 14 she won three Olympic golds, including the all-around title, at Montreal in 1976. She was the first gymnast ever to be awarded a perfect mark of 10.00 at the Olympics, which she achieved on the parallel bars.

Lewis ran the 100 m in Seoul in 9.92 seconds, winning gold after Ben Johnson was disqualified

33

Continued on next page

REDGRAVE AND PINSENT
At Atlanta 1996, the rower Steve Redgrave (left) won gold for the fourth Olympics in a row. It was his second win in the coxless pairs event with Matthew Pinsent. In 1988 he won the same event with Andrew Holmes, and in 1984 he won the coxed fours event. He will be going for gold number five at Sydney in the coxless fours.

Goggles were worn in the 1960s but no helmet

Ski poles are used for balance in turns

Two-piece outfit instead of the one-piece outfit worn by today's skiers

MARK SPITZ
Munich 1972 saw one of the greatest Olympic performances of all. The American swimmer Mark Spitz won all four individual events he entered – the 100 and 200 m freestyle and the 100 m and 200 m butterfly – all in world-record times. In winning three relay golds as well, he became the first athlete to win seven golds in one Olympics. He also won two relay golds in Mexico City in 1968.

Weissmuller was the first man to swim 109 yds (100 m) in less than 1 minute

JOHNNY WEISSMULLER
The American swimmer Johnny Weissmuller was most famous for his role of Tarzan in the series of films of the 1930s and 1940s. Before movie stardom he won five Olympic golds – three in 1924 (the 100 m and 400 m freestyle and the 800 m relay) and two in 1928 (the 100 m freestyle and the 800 m relay). He also won a bronze medal in 1924 as part of the U.S. water polo team.

Johnny Weissmuller as Tarzan

FANNY BLANKERS-KOEN
The Dutch sprinter Fanny Blankers-Koen was the most successful woman athlete at the London Olympics of 1948. She won gold in the 80 m hurdles, the 100 and 200 m, and the 4 x100 m relay. At the time, she held seven world records, including the long jump and high jump, neither of which she entered at the games. Mother of two, she was nicknamed "the flying housewife."

Winter Olympians

Heroes and heroines at the Winter Olympics include the ice-cool downhill skiers, the graceful and skilful ice skaters, the brave ski jumpers, and the determined cross-country skiers. A special place in Olympic history is reserved for the American speed skater Eric Heiden, who, in 1980, won gold in all five individual events, a feat never accomplished before or since.

Metal fasteners

Thick soles lock into bindings on the skis

Killy's ski boots of 1968

JEAN-CLAUDE KILLY
The French skier Jean-Claude Killy was brought up in the French ski resort of Val-d'Isère. At the age of 24 he won all three Alpine skiing golds (the downhill, slalom, and giant slalom) at the Grenoble Olympics in 1968. He became a member of the IOC in 1995.

Jean-Claude Killy carving a tight turn in the 1967 World Cup

Sonja Henie posing for the cameras

Katarina Witt's skimpy costumes in 1988 brought some criticism from the judges

KATARINA WITT
At the Calgary Winter Olympics of 1988, Katarina Witt, then competing for East Germany, took gold in the women's figure skating to retain the Olympic title she had won in Sarajevo four years earlier. She became the first skater since Sonja Henie to retain the title and was given a special award by the IOC.

Katarina Witt performing in the 1988 Olympics

SONJA HENIE
The Norwegian figure skater Sonja Henie was a child prodigy in figure skating. She won the Norwegian title aged just 10 and entered the 1924 Olympics aged 12. She won three successive Olympic golds in 1928, 1932, and 1936. She also won every world championship from 1927 to 1936, and went on to star in 11 Hollywood movies.

RAISA SMETANINA
The cross-country skier Raisa Smetanina is the top medal winner in the Winter Olympics. She won four gold medals, five silvers, and one bronze over four Olympiads between 1976 and 1988. She competed first for the U.S.S.R. and then for the Unified Team in 1992.

Getting fit

Performing at the Olympic Games is the dream of all athletes. When the chance comes, they must be at the top of their form so that they can give their best. For years, diet was not considered an important part of athletes' training programs. Now it is known that diet is as important as the shoes they wear. They must keep well hydrated and maintain stores of energy in their muscles. They must eat a balanced diet containing all the vitamins and minerals essential for good health. Shown here is a typical day's food that a decathlete in training needs to eat.

Large glass of water

8:00 A.M. – BREAKFAST
On waking, a decathlete would drink a large glass of water to rehydrate his body after the night. He would then have a small breakfast to keep him from feeling hungry during his early training session and to top up energy levels, especially his blood sugar. Vitamin C in the orange juice helps the body to absorb the iron in the cereal. Too little iron in the blood can lead to anemia.

0.25 pt (143 ml) semi-skimmed milk

1.4 oz (40 g high-energy balanced cereal

Orange juice

Stretching exercises warm up the muscles before training

9:00 - 11:30 A.M. – TRAINING
During a heavy training session, athletes must replace fluid lost through sweating because if they get dehydrated they will tire quickly and may risk injury. A large loss of fluid can affect their health. Isotonic sports drinks contain water, carbohydrates, and sodium and are effective at rehydrating the body, especially if fluid losses are great.

1.75 pt (1 liter) noncarbonated sports drink

Banned substances

Some athletes are so eager to win that they take drugs or special potions that make them stronger and faster. Not only is this cheating, but it can also be dangerous to the athletes' health. The use of "aids" such as performance-enhancing drugs and human growth hormones is therefore banned by international and national sports bodies.

0.88 pt (0.5 liter) noncarbonated sports drink

11:30 A.M. – MID-MORNING SNACK
Athletes have a big appetite because they need a lot of energy. They could not survive on only three meals a day, so they have snacks too. As soon as possible after a training session they eat food that is high in carbohydrates, such as bread and bananas, to refuel their muscles – lots of athletes eat while they are changing.

2 teaspoons of honey

Low-fat spread

Large banana, 4.2 oz (120 g) without skin

4 slices thick-sliced white bread, toasted

2 large glasses of water

2:00 P.M. – AFTERNOON MEAL
Athletes in training should have a meal early in the afternoon to allow time for the food to be digested before a run. The meal should contain carbohydrates, protein, and a little fat. Proteins and fats build and repair the body. An orange every day supplies a good intake of natural vitamin C. A diet should also include calcium for strong bones and teeth – milk, cheese, and yogurt are good sources. Some athletes feel that their diet does not contain enough vitamins and minerals, so they take supplements.

60 g (2 oz) Cheddar cheese

Large orange, 210 g (7.4 oz)

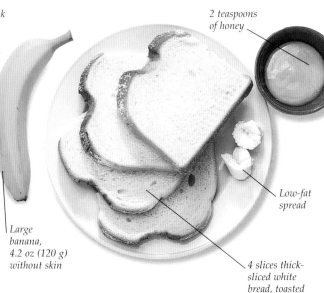

2 medium-size baked potatoes, 11.3 oz (320 g)

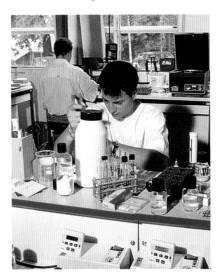

DRUG TESTING
Every medal winner at the Olympics has to give a urine sample, which is tested for banned substances in a laboratory. Athletes who use banned substances find better and better ways of hiding the fact, so drug-testing procedures have to improve too.

0.6 pt (330 ml) sports drink

4:00 P.M. – AFTERNOON SNACK
About an hour and a half before going for an evening run, an athlete would top up on fluid and carbohydrates. This chocolate bar is a good source of carbohydrates.

Chocolate bar

Large banana, 4.2 oz (120 g) without skin

The 1996 3000 m steeplechase silver medalist, Moses Kiptanui, running near his home in Kenya

5:30 - 6:30 P.M. – RUN
For an hour's run at low intensity, athletes would not carry a drink. In warm weather, they would probably take a water bottle or leave a drink somewhere en route.

Large glass of water

7:15 P.M. – EVENING MEAL
Soon after a run, an athlete has an evening meal. The food shown here is for a meal of stir-fry chicken with pasta and yogurt. As usual, it contains lots of carbohydrates, moderate amounts of protein, and some fat. The fruit and vegetables contain anti-oxidants, which can ward off illnesses like colds. These would affect an athlete's vital training schedule.

oz (200 g) chopped canned tomatoes

5.6 oz (160 g) sweet-and-sour sauce

:00 P.M. – EVENING SNACK
To make sure they do not go to bed hungry, athletes may have a sandwich and a hot drink about two hours after the evening meal. White bread is best because it is not so high in fiber as brown bread, and is therefore less bulky. Athletes have to be careful about how much fat they have during the day, because the body cannot easily turn fat into energy. They would therefore use a low-fat spread on the bread for their evening and midmorning snack, rather than butter.

5.3 oz (150 g) low-fat fruit yogurt

5.3 oz (150 g) breast of chicken without skin

Unlimited assorted vegetables

Large portion of pasta, 12.4 oz (350 g) cooked

Peanut butter

2 slices of thick-sliced white bread

Low-fat spread

Training

Athletes may compete for only a few minutes or even seconds. With the help of a coach, they train to be in peak condition at exactly the right time. Their aim is to perform to their best ability on the day, and if they are lucky, to win a medal.

WIND RESISTANCE
Technique is as important as fitness in competition. Athletes practice again and again, trying to reach perfection. In 1997, the British skier Graham Bell tested his downhill position for wind resistance in a wind tunnel made to test the wind resistance of Formula 1 cars.

WEIGHT TRAINING
Injury can mean months out of action and many more months of training to reach top condition again. The U.S. skier Picabo Street had her knee rebuilt after an accident but was determined to compete in the 1998 games. After hard work, she won gold in the giant slalom.

Mug of tea made with semi-skimmed milk

Shapes and sizes

JUST LIKE ALL human beings, sportsmen and women come in different shapes and sizes. For some sports, they develop a certain shape from training and competing, because the more a muscle is used, the more powerful and larger it becomes. For other sports, some natural shapes are more suitable than others. For example, a woman who stands 4 ft 10 in. (1.5 m) tall and weighs about 80 lb (38 kg) would not be good at shot putting, which needs strength and physical power. She would be better at gymnastics, which needs balance and agility.

WEIGHT LIFTER
Weight lifters develop powerful legs and shoulders. Their arms must not be too long or too short, because this makes it more difficult for them to lift the bar above their head. They have a compact body to maximize their strength and balance.

Arm muscles are used in the final stage of a lift

Wrist and fingers do a lot of work, so they are strong and supple

Side view of weight lifter

Gymnasts work in bare feet

Gymnasts must have complete muscle control

Strong legs are important for all the disciplines

Knee and ankle joints have to withstand sudden pressure as the lifter stands with the weight

The thick muscle in the buttocks, called the gluteus maximus, moves the legs

Feet have to support massive weights

The impact of running and jumping is absorbed by cushioning in the shoes

GYMNAST
Most gymnasts are fairly short and light to enable them to balance, bend, swing, and jump in the four disciplines. A gymnast uses the whole body to make shapes, so gymnasts must be strong and supple all over.

Swimmers wear caps to cut down resistance

Deltoid muscle lifts the arm

SPEED SKATER
Speed skaters use the leg muscles more than any others, so their legs and buttocks become well developed. Long arms help them to balance as they skate around the bends, and powerful shoulders help to pump the arms when extra speed is needed.

Pectoral muscle helps move the shoulder

Biceps and triceps bend and straighten the elbow

Strong lungs help swimmers to hold their breath underwater for as long as possible

ALL-AROUND ATHLETE
A decathlete has to be good at 10 different events. He needs to develop strength, speed, agility, and endurance and not concentrate on the attributes needed for one discipline. For example, he must not increase his body weight just to help him in the shot put, because too much weight would slow him down in the speed events.

Strong stomach muscles help the rest of the body to work

Strong upper leg for kicking through the water

Strong, flexible shoulders are needed for throwing the javelin

SWIMMER
Water resistance is much greater than air resistance, and it takes strength to push through water. Competition swimmers therefore have strong muscles in the upper back that lift the arms and move the shoulders. Muscles in the upper legs bend and straighten the knees and hips.

Muscles in the waist, abdomen, and lower back link the movements of the upper and lower body and are used in all athletics

Hamstring muscles in the back of the leg straighten the hip and bend the knee. A pulled or torn hamstring is one of the most common injuries in athletics.

The muscle in the calf bends the foot down when the athlete runs

Changing styles

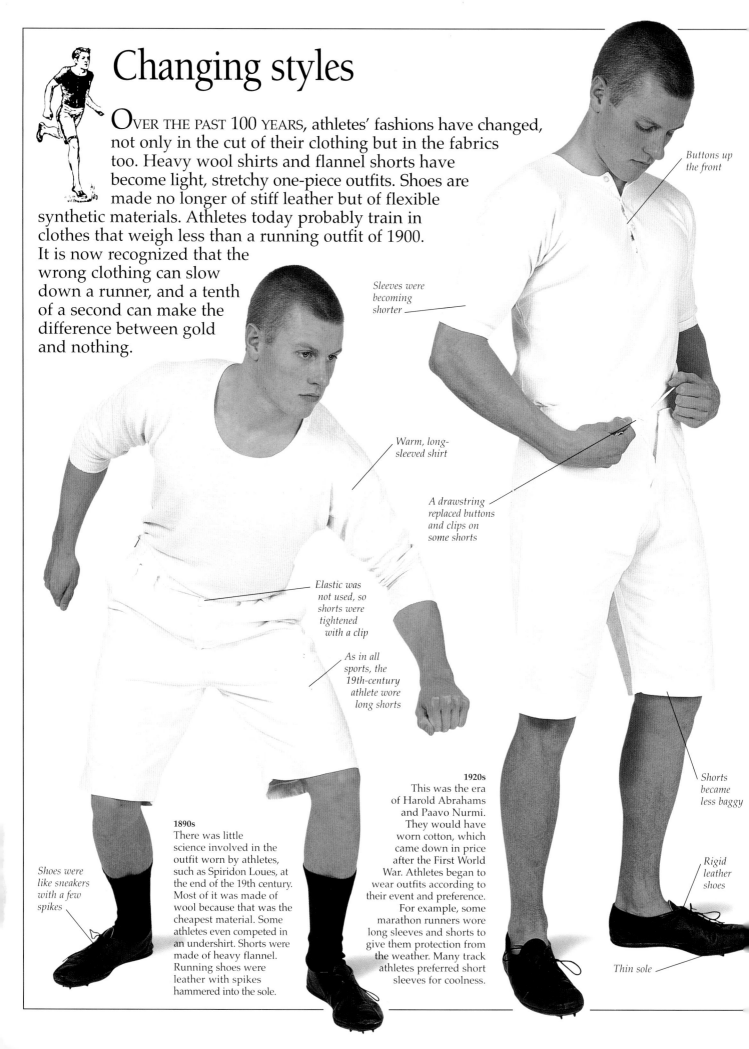

OVER THE PAST 100 YEARS, athletes' fashions have changed, not only in the cut of their clothing but in the fabrics too. Heavy wool shirts and flannel shorts have become light, stretchy one-piece outfits. Shoes are made no longer of stiff leather but of flexible synthetic materials. Athletes today probably train in clothes that weigh less than a running outfit of 1900. It is now recognized that the wrong clothing can slow down a runner, and a tenth of a second can make the difference between gold and nothing.

Buttons up the front

Sleeves were becoming shorter

Warm, long-sleeved shirt

A drawstring replaced buttons and clips on some shorts

Elastic was not used, so shorts were tightened with a clip

As in all sports, the 19th-century athlete wore long shorts

Shorts became less baggy

1920s
This was the era of Harold Abrahams and Paavo Nurmi. They would have worn cotton, which came down in price after the First World War. Athletes began to wear outfits according to their event and preference. For example, some marathon runners wore long sleeves and shorts to give them protection from the weather. Many track athletes preferred short sleeves for coolness.

1890s
There was little science involved in the outfit worn by athletes, such as Spiridon Loues, at the end of the 19th century. Most of it was made of wool because that was the cheapest material. Some athletes even competed in an undershirt. Shorts were made of heavy flannel. Running shoes were leather with spikes hammered into the sole.

Shoes were like sneakers with a few spikes

Rigid leather shoes

Thin sole

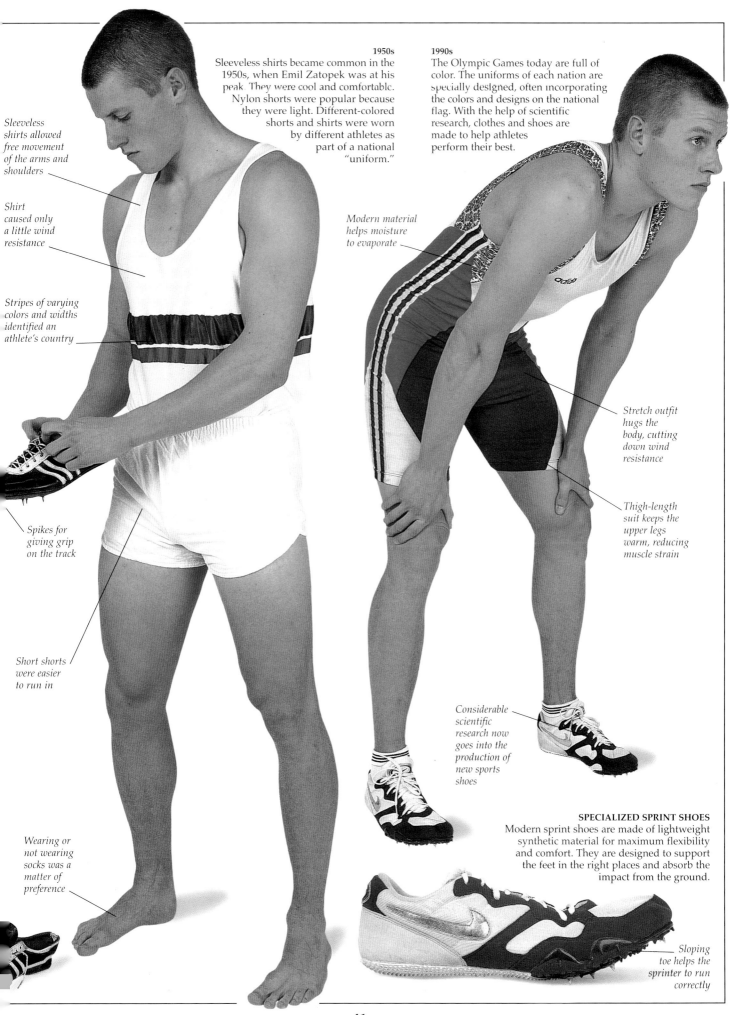

Sleeveless
shirts allowed
free movement
of the arms and
shoulders

Shirt
caused only
a little wind
resistance

Stripes of varying
colors and widths
identified an
athlete's country

Spikes for
giving grip
on the track

Short shorts
were easier
to run in

Wearing or
not wearing
socks was a
matter of
preference

1950s
Sleeveless shirts became common in the
1950s, when Emil Zatopek was at his
peak. They were cool and comfortable.
Nylon shorts were popular because
they were light. Different-colored
shorts and shirts were worn
by different athletes as
part of a national
"uniform."

1990s
The Olympic Games today are full of
color. The uniforms of each nation are
specially designed, often incorporating
the colors and designs on the national
flag. With the help of scientific
research, clothes and shoes are
made to help athletes
perform their best.

Modern material
helps moisture
to evaporate

Stretch outfit
hugs the
body, cutting
down wind
resistance

Thigh-length
suit keeps the
upper legs
warm, reducing
muscle strain

Considerable
scientific
research now
goes into the
production of
new sports
shoes

SPECIALIZED SPRINT SHOES
Modern sprint shoes are made of lightweight
synthetic material for maximum flexibility
and comfort. They are designed to support
the feet in the right places and absorb the
impact from the ground.

Sloping
toe helps the
sprinter to run
correctly

Made to measure

SAFETY IN SPORTS is important, but so too are speed and comfort. Designers today spend many hours of expensive research creating sports clothes that look good, give protection and comfort, and help athletes achieve great performances. They take advantage of research in other fields and have even used materials developed for use in space. Every sport has its own requirements. Some outfits must absorb impacts, some must be aerodynamic, others must be attractive. Improvements happen quickly, and today's athletes would be horrified by the clothes of just 10 years ago.

BASEBALL
Baseball catchers and the home plate umpire wear chest and head protection against deflections off the bat. These may come at 87 mph (140 km/h).

SWIMMING GOGGLES
Modern swimming goggles are shaped to fit tightly around the eyes so that they do not let in water or mist up. Swimmers wear goggles to protect their eyes from chlorine in the water and to allow them to see where they are going.

SWIMWEAR
This swimsuit of the 1920s may look similar to the blue one of the 1990s, but the two are in fact quite different. In the 1920s, swimsuits were made of cotton. They would have become heavy when wet and, because they did not fit tightly, would have slowed the swimmers down. Today, swimsuits are made to cling to the body and allow water to flow past quickly, helping swimmers to cut vital fractions of seconds off their race times.

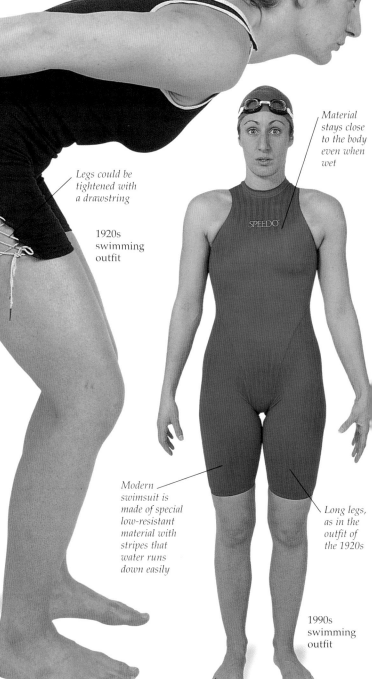

Material stays close to the body even when wet

Legs could be tightened with a drawstring

1920s swimming outfit

Mask protects the face from fast-traveling pucks

One glove has webbing between the fingers, while the stick hand has extra protection

These old-fashioned gloves do not have the same style of thumbs as modern gloves, which have been designed to prevent eye gouging

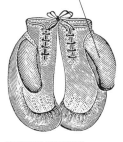

ICE HOCKEY PADDING
Ice hockey is the world's fastest team sport. The goalies wear huge pads on their legs and arms to protect them from the puck, which can be hit at more than 124 mph (200 km/h). They also wear masks that protect the head, neck, and throat.

BOXING GLOVES
Boxers wear gloves to protect the opponent. Big, heavy gloves absorb much of the power of punches before they hit the opponent and spread the impact of the blows. Before a fight, both boxers' gloves are weighed to make sure they are the same.

Modern swimsuit is made of special low-resistant material with stripes that water runs down easily

Long legs, as in the outfit of the 1920s

1990s swimming outfit

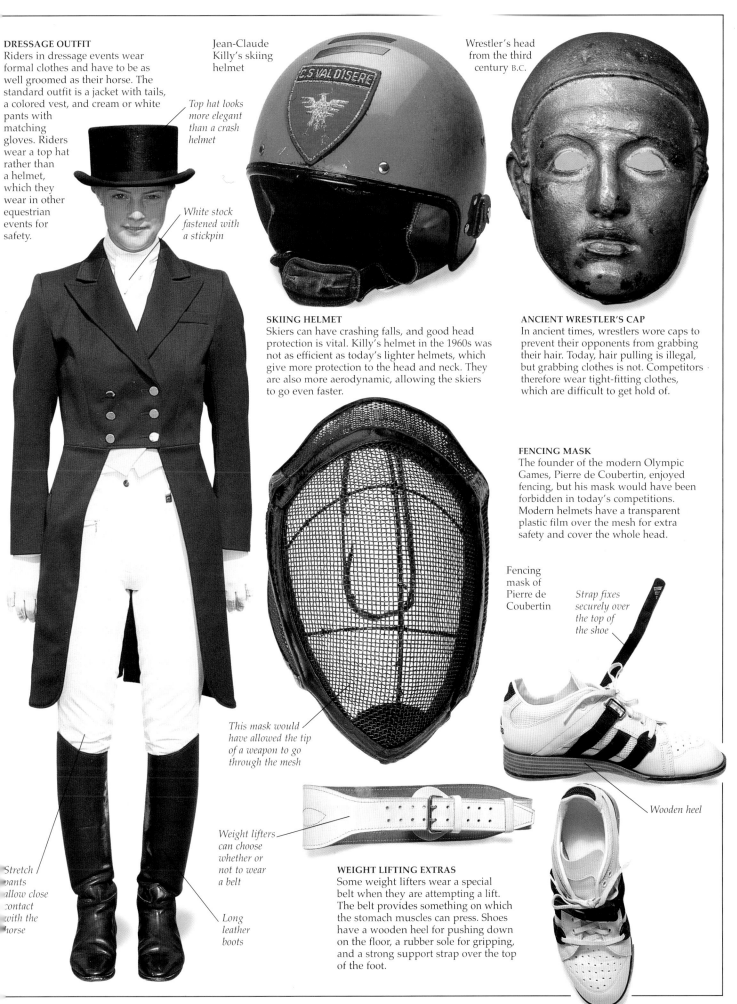

DRESSAGE OUTFIT

Riders in dressage events wear formal clothes and have to be as well groomed as their horse. The standard outfit is a jacket with tails, a colored vest, and cream or white pants with matching gloves. Riders wear a top hat rather than a helmet, which they wear in other equestrian events for safety.

Top hat looks more elegant than a crash helmet

White stock fastened with a stickpin

Stretch pants allow close contact with the horse

Long leather boots

Jean-Claude Killy's skiing helmet

C.S VALD'ISÈRE

Wrestler's head from the third century B.C.

SKIING HELMET

Skiers can have crashing falls, and good head protection is vital. Killy's helmet in the 1960s was not as efficient as today's lighter helmets, which give more protection to the head and neck. They are also more aerodynamic, allowing the skiers to go even faster.

ANCIENT WRESTLER'S CAP

In ancient times, wrestlers wore caps to prevent their opponents from grabbing their hair. Today, hair pulling is illegal, but grabbing clothes is not. Competitors therefore wear tight-fitting clothes, which are difficult to get hold of.

FENCING MASK

The founder of the modern Olympic Games, Pierre de Coubertin, enjoyed fencing, but his mask would have been forbidden in today's competitions. Modern helmets have a transparent plastic film over the mesh for extra safety and cover the whole head.

Fencing mask of Pierre de Coubertin

Strap fixes securely over the top of the shoe

This mask would have allowed the tip of a weapon to go through the mesh

Weight lifters can choose whether or not to wear a belt

Wooden heel

WEIGHT LIFTING EXTRAS

Some weight lifters wear a special belt when they are attempting a lift. The belt provides something on which the stomach muscles can press. Shoes have a wooden heel for pushing down on the floor, a rubber sole for gripping, and a strong support strap over the top of the foot.

Wheels of fortune

THE EQUIPMENT for wheel sports has probably changed more than any other equipment used in the Olympics. Advances in gears, tires, brakes, and lightweight materials, particularly over the last 20 years, have improved racing bicycles by leaps and bounds. Bicycles are now made specifically for different events, such as track racing, road racing, pursuit, and mountain biking. Modern racing wheelchairs have also taken advantage of these developments and, like racing bikes, look completely different from their "everyday" counterparts seen on the street.

A modern racing wheelchair weighs only about 18 lb (8 kg)

Steering can be set up to make the chair go around a track perfectly in one lane

Tires are 0.75 in (19 mm) wide

Athlete "punches" the outside ring around to move the chair forward

MODERN RACING WHEELCHAIR
Racing wheelchairs have developed from standard upright chairs, through long, four-wheeled chairs to the modern three-wheeled "chariots." Before a race, each chair is checked by officials to make sure its specifications, such as length and size of wheels, fall within the regulations.

High handlebars would have put the rider in a wind-resistant, upright position

Metal frame

Thick tires would have gripped well but would have made the bike slow

1890s
Bicycles used in the first Olympic Games must have been uncomfortable to ride. The handlebars were at the same height as the saddle with little space in the middle, so the rider would have been rather cramped, with his weight over the back wheel. This bike has only one gear and no brakes – like track racing bicycles today.

Hard leather saddle offered little comfort

Drop handlebars with brake levers

Wheels were fixed with an early, quick-release mechanism

The bike had three gears

1930s
Bicycles gradually became more streamlined. The horizontal crossbar and longer wheelbase of this bike allowed the rider to take up a less wind-resistant position and made pedaling easier and more efficient.

Toe straps kept the rider's feet on the pedals

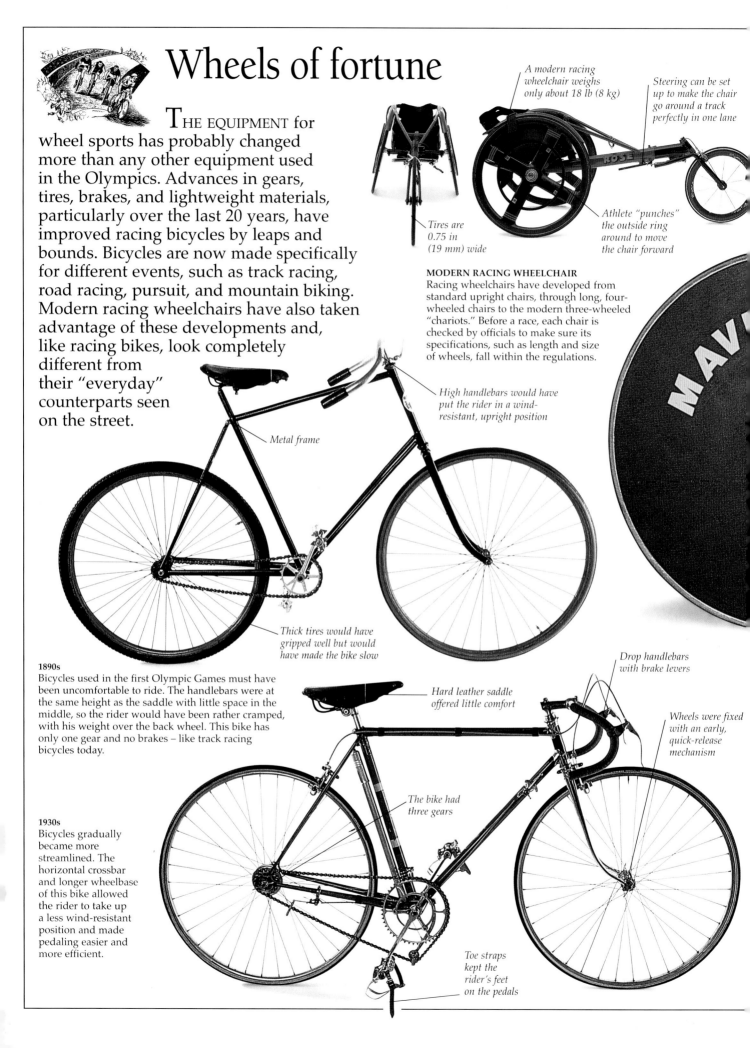

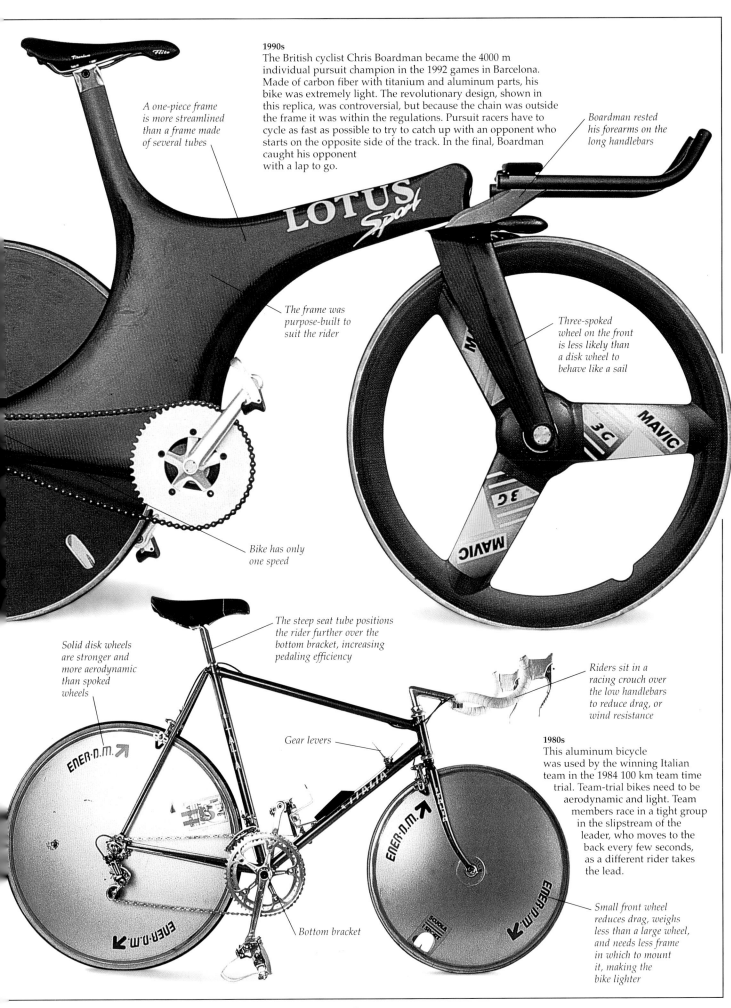

1990s
The British cyclist Chris Boardman became the 4000 m individual pursuit champion in the 1992 games in Barcelona. Made of carbon fiber with titanium and aluminum parts, his bike was extremely light. The revolutionary design, shown in this replica, was controversial, but because the chain was outside the frame it was within the regulations. Pursuit racers have to cycle as fast as possible to try to catch up with an opponent who starts on the opposite side of the track. In the final, Boardman caught his opponent with a lap to go.

A one-piece frame is more streamlined than a frame made of several tubes

Boardman rested his forearms on the long handlebars

The frame was purpose-built to suit the rider

Three-spoked wheel on the front is less likely than a disk wheel to behave like a sail

Bike has only one speed

The steep seat tube positions the rider further over the bottom bracket, increasing pedaling efficiency

Solid disk wheels are stronger and more aerodynamic than spoked wheels

Riders sit in a racing crouch over the low handlebars to reduce drag, or wind resistance

Gear levers

1980s
This aluminum bicycle was used by the winning Italian team in the 1984 100 km team time trial. Team-trial bikes need to be aerodynamic and light. Team members race in a tight group in the slipstream of the leader, who moves to the back every few seconds, as a different rider takes the lead.

Bottom bracket

Small front wheel reduces drag, weighs less than a large wheel, and needs less frame in which to mount it, making the bike lighter

Skates and skis

THE EQUIPMENT USED IN the first Winter Olympic Games in 1924 at Chamonix, France, is almost unrecognizable compared with that used at the dawn of the 21st century. Light, strong, synthetic materials, such as fiberglass, have been developed to replace wood and iron. Leather skating boots have become softer and more comfortable without losing their support. Winter sports can be dangerous, and equipment is now designed with safety in mind as much as speed. Skiers, skaters, and bobsled riders go much faster than their early counterparts, but they face far less risk of injury or death.

Shoe is fixed to the blade with leather and metal

FIRST EVENT
The men's speed skating 500 m was the first event to be decided in the first Winter Olympic Games in 1924. The blade on this early skate is curved up at the toe. This curve was removed on later speed skates.

RAISED ON HIGH
Speed skating takes place on an oval track. The two skaters have to swap lanes along the back straight of each lap to make sure they both skate the correct distance. The boot of this early speed skate is raised above the blade. This allowed the skater to lean inward around the corners.

Long single-edged blade helped the skater to start quickly and maintain high speed

Boot is fixed to metal struts on the blade

Early wooden ski

Fiberglass ski, pre-195

Speed skating

Traditional speed skating is a graceful sport, with the skaters taking smooth, powerful strokes. They race against the clock at speeds of up to 34 mph (56 km/h). Short-track speed skating is more aggressive because the skaters race against each other.

Boot has Velcro fastenings

SPEED SKATER
Speed skaters race in one direction around a track. They do not need to perform any special movements

SHORT-TRACK SPEED SKATE
This short-track speed skate was used in 1988 when the sport was demonstrated at the Winter Olympics. Short-track speed skating was an Olympic competition sport for the first time in 1992 at Albertville, France.

Blade made of steel

To reduce wind resistance, the crew members keep their heads below the sides of the sled

Sled is made of wood

EARLY BOBSLED
Bobsleds were invented in the 1880s, when someone lashed two toboggans together. The first Olympic four-man bobsled competition was held in 1924. A two-man event was first held in 1932.

Bobsledding
There are very few sights in sport as spectacular as a bobsled on the run. Early sleds were open, and the driver steered using a wheel at the front. Riders today are well protected inside the sled.

MODERN BOBSLED
Bobsleds today hurtle down a run at speeds of up to 93 mph (150 km/h). Made of carbon fiber, they are light and aerodynamic. Two-man bobs must not exceed 8.8 ft (2.7 m) in length and 860 lb (390 kg) in weight, including the riders. The limits for four-man bobs are 12.5 ft (3.8 m) and 1,389 lb (630 kg).

Figure skating
The blades on figure skates are hollow-ground to give them an inside and outside edge. They are curved slightly to allow the skaters to change their weight from front to back. All the movements that figure skaters perform rely on these four basic edges.

HIGH JUMPER
The high top of this 1950s figure skate gave a skater ankle support but offered little flexibility. It was in the 1952 Olympics that the American Dick Button showed the world his new jump – the triple loop – which is now a popular jump for men and women.

Leather upper

Fiberglass
ski, pre-1980

Fiberglass
ski, 1990s

Fiberglass
ski, 1990s

SKIS THROUGH THE AGES
Ski bindings attach the skis to a skier's boots. They have changed enormously since the first Olympic Alpine skiing event in 1936, as have the skis themselves. Early skis were wooden and had a leather strap that buckled around the boots. Today's fiberglass skis have clip bindings that release the boot in a fall.

FIGURE SKATER
Blades for figure skating are designed to allow the skaters to skate in circles, turn, jump, and spin. The skaters move their weight to use the edges.

Serrated section is called a toe rake and is used in toe jumps and toe stops

1990s
Modern ice skates are much more comfortable than early ones. This 1990s skate is almost seven times lighter than the 1950s one. Boots can now be different colors to match the skater's costume.

Fancy footwork

A GOOD PAIR OF SHOES is one of the most important items of sports equipment. Shoes do not just protect the feet but can cut down the stresses on ankle and knee joints too. Olympic athletes today know that not only will they reduce injuries by wearing the right shoes, but their performance will be improved too. A great deal of research and development now goes into the production of a new model of sports shoe, and better materials and shapes are being discovered all the time. This makes the shoes expensive, but being an Olympic athlete does not come cheap.

Sports shoes

Sports shoes are designed especially for different games. Players who have to run fast, make sudden stops, or kick a ball all require different things from their shoes. Conditions also affect shoe design. For example, basketball shoes would be useless on a muddy soccer field, and soccer shoes would be dangerous on a clay tennis court.

Perforations let air in and heat out, keeping the feet cool

TENNIS SHOE
Tennis players need shoes with a good grip because they have to stop and change direction quickly. Cushioning in the soles protects the feet from the constant jarring caused by running on a hard surface.

SOCCER SHOE
Soccer players need to feel the ball through their shoes and have support for their ankles. Good soccer shoes are therefore made of soft, flexible leather. They allow players to kick the ball with the inside and the outside of their feet. Studs can be changed for different surface conditions.

Soles have grip to prevent the athlete from slipping

RUNNING SHOE (ABOVE)
Each running step uses three times as much force as a walking step. Running shoes have compressed-air shock absorbers in the midsole to reduce stress-related injuries to the foot. Outside conditions can damage the midsole, so some running shoes have "sell-by" dates.

JAVELIN SHOE (LEFT)
Javelin throwers wear a different shoe on each foot, depending on from which one they throw. The athletes land heavily on the heel of one foot just before throwing and then have to stop quickly in front of the foul line. The shoes are tough, with good ankle support and padding around the toe.

Basketball shoe

This modern basketball shoe has been broken down into its many components, each one designed carefully to provide comfort and support to different parts of the foot. The three main components are the upper, the midsole, and the outsole.

Flexible frame for the ankle wrap

High, padded he gives all-around protection to the back of the foot

Ankle wrap provides ankle stability

PLAYING THE GAME
Basketball players are required to sprint, stop sharply, turn, and of course jump. The match shown here is United States versus Lithuania at Atlanta in 1996. The Lithuanians, in white, eventually won the bronze medal, while the Americans went on to win gold, as expected.

HEEL AND ANKLE PROTECTION
Playing basketball puts great strain on the feet and legs, especially the ankle joints. The heel and ankle area of a basketball shoe must therefore provide support and protection. It must fit perfectly around the heel to prevent blisters as well as more serious injuries.

Tongue extends up the shin for extra support

Soft padding for comfort

Loop can be used to pull on the shoe

Holes for laces

Elastic straps are stitched to the inside of the shoe

UPPER
The upper part of the shoe covers the top of the foot and goes around the side of the foot as far as the ankle. It is made of lightweight synthetic material that allows the foot to breathe inside the shoe.

AS A WHOLE
Many years were spent testing and developing this shoe before it was put into production. Each section was developed by scientists with the help of top players. When all the components are put together, they form a lightweight, top-of-the-range basketball shoe that provides support and freedom of movement – and looks good too.

Midsole

Fluid capsule visible through a "window" in the sole

Heel stabilizer containing cushioning fluid

Lightweight sock liner

Midsole is reinforced to provide stability

Midsole is shaped to fit the contours of the foot

Capsule containing special fluid provides cushioning and stability underneath the heel and ball of the foot

Fluid capsule fits into a recess in the midsole

OUTSOLE
Basketball is played indoors on a smooth wooden court. The rubber tread on the bottom of the sole provides the vital grip players need to prevent them from slipping as they stop and turn quickly.

Rubber outsole

Perfect timing

I<small>T WILL TAKE LONGER FOR YOU</small> to read this paragraph than it will take the winners of the men's and women's Olympic 100 m finals to run their race. The time for the men's 100 m is now less than 10 seconds. The improvement in athletes' technique and fitness has helped them to achieve record-breaking performances, but technology has helped too, in the development of synthetic tracks, aerodynamic clothes, and modern shoes. Starting and timing methods have had to keep up, and modern electronic systems help both athletes and officials, by ensuring that every race is as fair as possible.

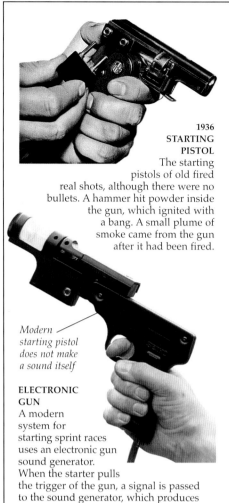

1936 STARTING PISTOL
The starting pistols of old fired real shots, although there were no bullets. A hammer hit powder inside the gun, which ignited with a bang. A small plume of smoke came from the gun after it had been fired.

Modern starting pistol does not make a sound itself

ELECTRONIC GUN
A modern system for starting sprint races uses an electronic gun sound generator. When the starter pulls the trigger of the gun, a signal is passed to the sound generator, which produces a sound and transmits it by cable to a loudspeaker built into the back of each starting block. This ensures that all the athletes hear the signal at the same time.

STARTING BLOCKS
Electronic starting blocks were introduced in the 1980s. Pressure exerted by athletes on the blocks is measured and relayed to the starter. The most advanced system monitors each athlete individually, taking into account weight, sex, and experience. It can tell the difference between a non-deliberate movement and a false start.

100 M RECORDS
Since 1896, the winning time of the men's Olympic 100 m final has improved by more than 2 seconds. The first women's 100 m took place in 1928, and their time has improved by slightly less.

The start

The start of a race must be fair. Runners in the outside lanes used to be at a disadvantage because the sound of the gun reached them after it reached the inside athlete. Improved starting systems have now eliminated this problem.

ANCIENT START
This is the marble starting sill used in the Pythian Games at Delphi in the 5th century B.C. Ancient Greek runners used a standing start with their arms stretched forward. They gripped the grooves in the sill firmly with their toes.

Olympic tracks were made of cinder until 1968

Athletes used a trowel to dig a hole in the track behind the starting line

PREPARING FOR THE 100 M IN 1928
Starting blocks as we know them were first authorized in 1938, which meant that they could not be used at the Olympic Games until 1948. Before then, athletes in sprint races dug holes in the track to give them something to push against at the start.

	1896	1900	1908	1924	1928	1936
MEN	T. Burke (USA) 12.0	F. Jarvis (USA) 11.0	R. Walker (S. Afr.) 10.8	H. Abrahams (GB) 10.6	P. Williams (Can.) 10.8	J. Owens (USA) 10.3
WOMEN	-	-	-	-	E. Robinson (USA) 12.2	H. Stephens (USA 11.5

CHRONOMETER

In the early part of the 20th century, athletes were timed using a chronometer. This one has three dials fixed to the outside of the box. The dials record hours, minutes, and seconds.

Wooden box contains the chronometer's mechanism

The finish of the 100 m in Tokyo in 1964

100 M FINISH 1964

In 1964, an electronic quartz timing system was used at the Olympic Games for the first time. It measured time more accurately than anything that had been used before, and led to the launch of the first quartz watches in 1969. Many timing judges sat at the finish line, each with his or her own stopwatch.

Quartz sports timer used in 1964

The finish

Athletes and spectators no longer have to wait agonizing seconds to find out who has won which medal. With modern technology, they can learn the placings almost immediately. Athletes can now be timed to within a thousandth of a second.

SLIT-VIDEO FINISH

A new slit-video system now makes it easier than ever before for judges to decide on the winner of the 100 m. The system scans a thin line aligned with the finishing line up to 2,000 times per second, forming a clear image of the athletes crossing the line.

COMPUTER JUDGES

With the slit-video photo-finish system, an image of athletes on the line is immediately displayed on monitors for the judges to study. They move a cursor to the torso of each athlete and read the time from a scale at the bottom of the image. Color images make it even easier for judges to pick out each athlete.

1948	1952	1960	1968	1976	1984	1992	1996
H. Dillard (USA) 10.3	L. Remigino (USA) 10.4	A. Hary (W. Ger.) 10.32	J. Hines (USA) 9.95	H. Crawford (Trin.) 10.06	C. Lewis (USA) 9.99	L. Christie (GB) 9.96	D. Bailey (Can.) 9.84
Blankers-Koen (Neth.) 11.9	M. Jackson (Aus.) 11.5	W. Rudolph (USA) 11.18	W. Tyus (USA) 11.08	A. Richter (W. Ger.) 11.08	E. Ashford (USA) 10.97	G. Devers (USA) 10.82	G. Devers (USA) 10.94

Spoilsports

THE OLYMPIC GAMES are major media events and attract international audiences of millions. They therefore present people with an ideal opportunity to bring their protests and grievances to the attention of the whole world. There have been very few Summer Olympic Games that have not been affected by international or national politics, and in most cases it is the athletes who have lost out. For almost every Summer Games, the politicians of at least one country have withdrawn their team. Other countries have been excluded from some games by the organizers. The games of 1916, 1940, and 1944 did not take place at all because of world wars.

Swastika was used as the symbol of the Nazi party

Commemorative medal

JAPAN AS HOST
It took almost 20 years for Japan to be fully taken back into the Olympic fold after the Second World War. The choice of Tokyo as host for the 1964 games showed that the IOC thought Japan had been shunned for long enough, but it was an unpopular choice with many people who remembered the war.

Hitler's soldiers invaded Poland in September 1939, causing Britain and France to declare war on Germany

Statuette of a German Nazi

SIGN OF SUPPORT
American athletes Tommie Smith and John Carlos came first and third in the 1968 men's 200 m. At the medal ceremony, they showed their support for the Black Power movement's racial equality campaign in America by raising black-gloved clenched fists during the playing of their anthem. They were expelled from the Olympic village.

THE GREAT WAR
The games of 1916 were due to be held in Berlin, Germany, but when war broke out in 1914, they had to be canceled. The first games to be held after the First World War were in Antwerp, Belgium, in 1920. Germany, Austria, Hungary, and Turkey were not invited because of their part in the war. Antwerp had been occupied by enemy forces only 18 months before the games began, but the organizing committee still put on a successful games with a record number of countries and competitors attending.

Antwerp city's badge

Many Olympic Games posters depicted ancient Greek athletes

Poster advertising the Antwerp games

VIIᵉ OLYMPIADE ANVERS (BELGIQUE) AOÛT-SEPTEMBRE 1920

NAZI PROPAGANDA
The games of 1936 were held in Berlin, Germany. Adolf Hitler used the games as a Nazi propaganda exercise. He hoped that blond, blue-eyed, pale-skinned Aryan athletes would win everything, but black Americans won most of the athletics medals. War broke out in 1939, and the games were not held again until 1948.

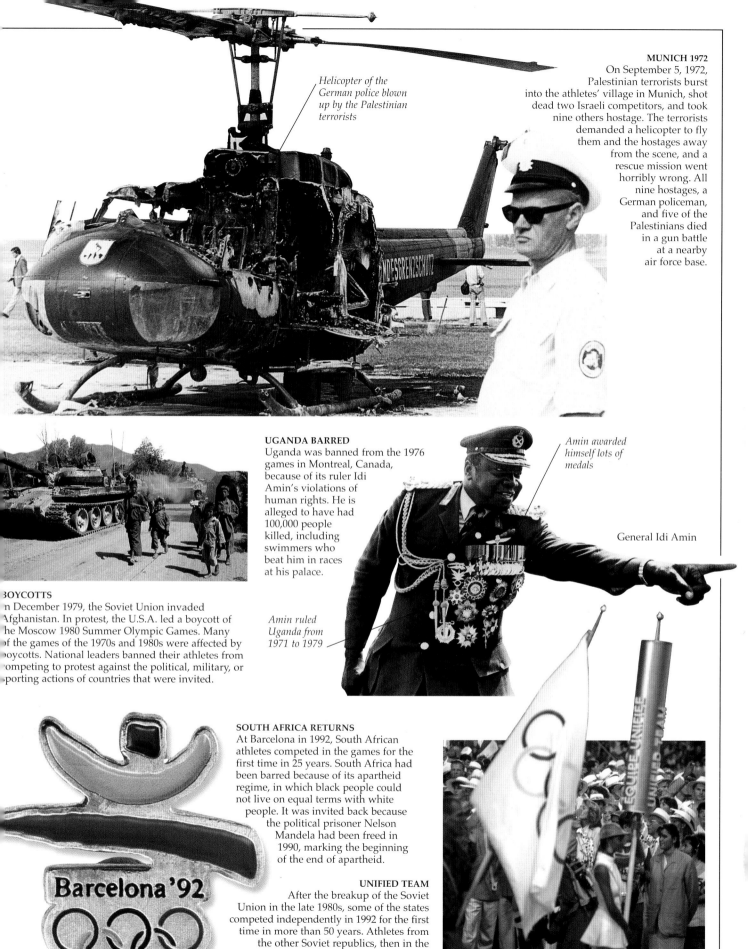

Helicopter of the German police blown up by the Palestinian terrorists

MUNICH 1972
On September 5, 1972, Palestinian terrorists burst into the athletes' village in Munich, shot dead two Israeli competitors, and took nine others hostage. The terrorists demanded a helicopter to fly them and the hostages away from the scene, and a rescue mission went horribly wrong. All nine hostages, a German policeman, and five of the Palestinians died in a gun battle at a nearby air force base.

UGANDA BARRED
Uganda was banned from the 1976 games in Montreal, Canada, because of its ruler Idi Amin's violations of human rights. He is alleged to have had 100,000 people killed, including swimmers who beat him in races at his palace.

Amin awarded himself lots of medals

General Idi Amin

Amin ruled Uganda from 1971 to 1979

BOYCOTTS
In December 1979, the Soviet Union invaded Afghanistan. In protest, the U.S.A. led a boycott of the Moscow 1980 Summer Olympic Games. Many of the games of the 1970s and 1980s were affected by boycotts. National leaders banned their athletes from competing to protest against the political, military, or sporting actions of countries that were invited.

SOUTH AFRICA RETURNS
At Barcelona in 1992, South African athletes competed in the games for the first time in 25 years. South Africa had been barred because of its apartheid regime, in which black people could not live on equal terms with white people. It was invited back because the political prisoner Nelson Mandela had been freed in 1990, marking the beginning of the end of apartheid.

UNIFIED TEAM
After the breakup of the Soviet Union in the late 1980s, some of the states competed independently in 1992 for the first time in more than 50 years. Athletes from the other Soviet republics, then in the Commonwealth of Independent States, competed as the Unified Team and paraded under the Olympic flag. The team finished second in the winter medals table and top in the summer.

Souvenir pin from Barcelona 1992

Behind the scenes

ON SEPTEMBER 23, 1993, Juan Antonio Samaranch, president of the IOC, announced that Sydney had won the right to host the games of the XXVII Olympiad. The Olympic Games are the biggest sporting event in the world, and hosting them is an enormous undertaking. As well as the competitions, the organizing committee must arrange transport, accommodation, and security for thousands of people. More than 10,000 competitors and 5,000 support staff from 200 countries attend the games. Up to 15,000 journalists come to cover the events. The city must also prepare itself for the arrival of tens of thousands of spectators from all over the world. All this costs money, and since 1984, the Olympic movement has allowed host cities to meet the costs with the help of advertising and sponsorship.

A WINNING BID
The Australian delegation cheered when the IOC awarded the 2000 games to Sydney. Several cities bid for each games. Members of the IOC consider the bids, then meet to vote seven years before the games will be held. One bid has to gain more than half of the votes to win.

THE SITES
Sydney's Olympic plan involved the development of four world-class sporting facilities based on four Olympic precincts including Sydney Olympic Park, shown here under construction. Adequate transport for spectators is vital. Trains and buses will be able to carry nearly 80,000 spectators an hour to new terminals only a short walk away from where most sports will be.

Weight lifting

Sailing

The Olympic rings can be used only on official Olympic items

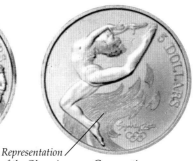
Gymnastics

Representation of the Olympic flame

Field hockey

Archery

Athletics

COMMEMORATIVE COINS
The design and production of commemorative items such as coins, medals, and buttons has to be organized well in advance of the games. These six coins are from a series of coins cut to celebrate the Sydney games. Each one has been designed to represent a different sport. They may be valuable collectors' items in a few years' time.

HOUSING THE ATHLETES
This is the 1998 Olympic "village" for athletes in Nagano. The first village was in Los Angeles in 1932, but it was for men only. In 2000, all athletes will live together in one village for the first time in Olympic history. After the Olympics it will be converted to accommodate 7,000 competitors and officials for the Paralympics. More ramps will be built for wheelchair access, and Braille instructions and signs will be added.

54

PARIS 1924

VIIIᵉ OLYMPIADE

JEUX OLYMPIQUES

THE CEREMONIES

After each final, the athletes who were first, second, and third receive their medals in a special ceremony. The organizing committee must devise the ceremony and make sure that enough medals have been made. The flags and national anthems of all competing nations have to be available.

The Intelsat 7 satellites provide up to 90,000 voice channels and three TV broadcasts simultaneously

Poster for the 1924 Olympic Games in Paris

Dish reflects radio signals from one place to another

MEDIA COVERAGE

The Olympic Games have a worldwide audience of more than 3.5 billion people. The launching of satellites in space has meant that the events can be filmed and shown live around the world. Written reports and photographs are now sent through "cyberspace" on the Internet or along telephone lines as faxes.

ADVERTISING THE GAMES

Today, there is probably little need to advertise the games, but organizing committees still have an advertising budget. At least one poster has been designed for every games since 1896, and the same design has often been used on the official programs.

Button from the 1912 Olympic Games

Buttons are sometimes presented to those who have helped at the games

Olympiska Spelen Stockholm 1912

INTERNATIONAL OLYMPIC COMMITTEE

The IOC consists of people who sit on their own country's Olympic committee. The president of the IOC is one of the most important people in the world of sport. Avery Brundage (left) was president of the IOC in 1972 when terrorists attacked the athletes' village in Munich. After the tragedy he made a speech to say that the games must go on after a 24-hour break.

THE START OF THINGS TO COME

The Stockholm Olympics of 1912 was one of the two or three best ever and showed the hosts of future games how it should be done. The organizing committee drew up a full list of events, trained the officials thoroughly, and introduced the use of electric timing devices and public-address systems.

The stadium

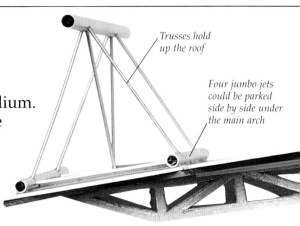

Trusses hold up the roof

Four jumbo jets could be parked side by side under the main arch

THE CENTERPIECE OF ANY OLYMPIC city is the main stadium. For most Summer Olympic and Paralympic Games, the stadium hosts the opening and closing ceremonies and the track and field events, including the marathon finish. Sports architects have to consider many different aspects when designing a new stadium. There can be more than 100,000 spectators plus thousands of journalists, athletes, and staff in a stadium at any one time. Safety, crowd flow, comfort, and services in all areas of the stadium have to be considered. The architects use computers to identify any possible problems raised by a design. The computers can even show the view from individual seats before the stadium is built.

THE PLAYERS' TUNNEL
Marching into the Olympic stadium must be a thrilling experience. Ancient Greek athletes would have experienced much the same feeling as they walked up this tunnel to emerge into the stadium at Olympia. The tunnel was 35 yd (32 m) long.

MUNICH STADIUM
Hosting the games gives cities an excuse to build magnificent new stadiums. Munich's Olympic Stadium was built for the 1972 games. It can hold 80,000 spectators. Two years after the games, soccer's World Cup Final was held there.

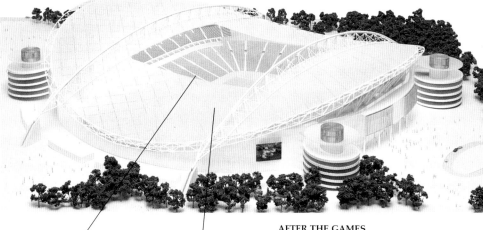

Seats in the lower tier will be moved to form a rectangle around a rugby field, for example

In post-Olympic mode, a polycarbonate roof will provide cover for 60,000 seats

AFTER THE GAMES
The Sydney Olympic stadium will be used for rugby and other sports after the Olympics and Paralympics. Two temporary stands at the north and south will be removed, reducing the seating capacity by 30,000. This model shows how it will look.

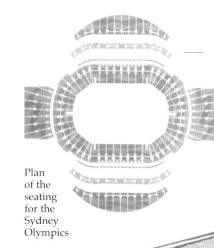

Plan of the seating for the Sydney Olympics

The Olympic soccer final will be played on the grass infield

The running track is lower than the front row of seats

18,000 trucks were required to deliver the concrete for the superstructure of the stadium

Athletes enter the arena along a passage between blocks of seats

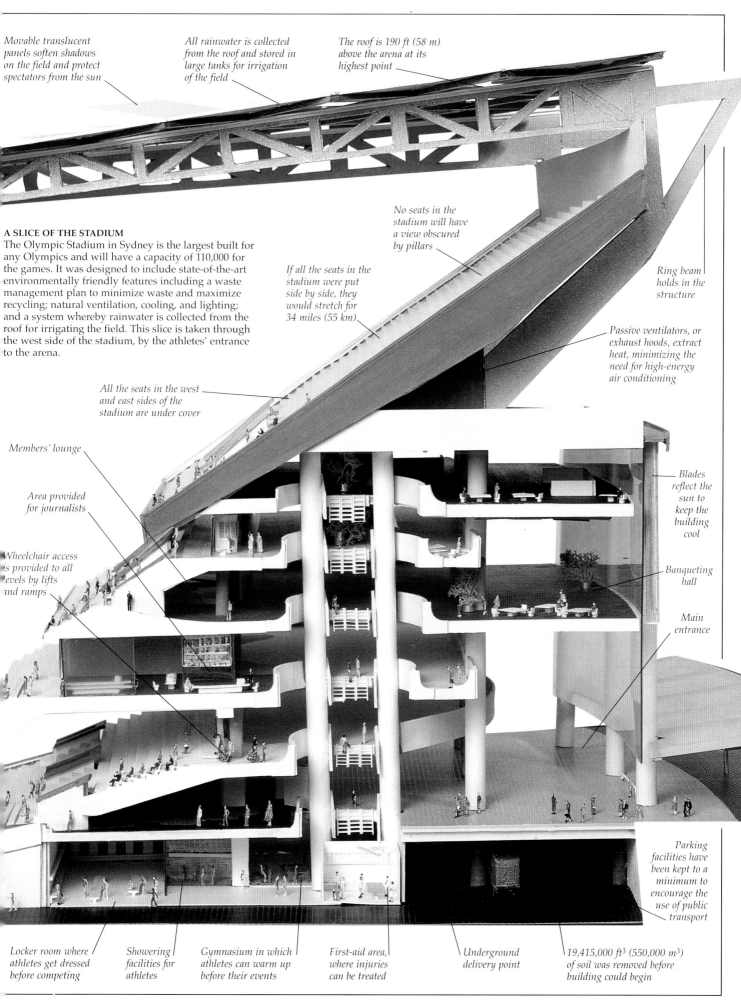

Movable translucent panels soften shadows on the field and protect spectators from the sun

All rainwater is collected from the roof and stored in large tanks for irrigation of the field

The roof is 190 ft (58 m) above the arena at its highest point

A SLICE OF THE STADIUM
The Olympic Stadium in Sydney is the largest built for any Olympics and will have a capacity of 110,000 for the games. It was designed to include state-of-the-art environmentally friendly features including a waste management plan to minimize waste and maximize recycling; natural ventilation, cooling, and lighting; and a system whereby rainwater is collected from the roof for irrigating the field. This slice is taken through the west side of the stadium, by the athletes' entrance to the arena.

No seats in the stadium will have a view obscured by pillars

If all the seats in the stadium were put side by side, they would stretch for 34 miles (55 km)

Ring beam holds in the structure

Passive ventilators, or exhaust hoods, extract heat, minimizing the need for high-energy air conditioning

All the seats in the west and east sides of the stadium are under cover

Members' lounge

Area provided for journalists

Wheelchair access is provided to all levels by lifts and ramps

Blades reflect the sun to keep the building cool

Banqueting hall

Main entrance

Parking facilities have been kept to a minimum to encourage the use of public transport

Locker room where athletes get dressed before competing

Showering facilities for athletes

Gymnasium in which athletes can warm up before their events

First-aid area, where injuries can be treated

Underground delivery point

19,415,000 ft³ (550,000 m³) of soil was removed before building could begin

Into the future

PREDICTING THE FUTURE in the Olympic Games is a difficult task. Future sites are known seven years in advance, but no one can say for certain which athletes will compete there or who the medal winners will be. Now that the Winter and Summer Olympics are held in separate years, sports fans have to wait for only two years to cheer home new heroes. Millions of spectators worldwide will watch the events unfold. There will be triumphs and disasters, controversies and record-breaking performances. Whatever happens, athletes will remember that "the important thing is not winning the race, but taking part."

There will be 28 sports at the Sydney 2000 Summer Olympic Games.

AQUATICS	GYMNASTICS
Diving	Artistic
Swimming	Rhythmic
Synchronized	Trampolining
swimming	
Water polo	HANDBALL
	HOCKEY
ARCHERY	JUDO
ATHLETICS	MODERN
BADMINTON	PENTATHLON
BASEBALL	ROWING
BASKETBALL	SAILING
BOXING	SHOOTING
CANOE/KAYAK	SOCCER
Slalom	
Sprint	
CYCLING	
Mountain bike	
Road	
Track	
EQUESTRIAN	
Dressage	
Show jumping	
Three-day event	
FENCING	

MICHAEL JOHNSON
In Atlanta in 1996, Michael Johnson won the 200 and 400 m. He has kept his form since winning both events, and he will be a strong favorite to win at least one race, if not both races, in Sydney. Although Johnson's erect running style is not one that coaches recommend, his success proves there is no correct way to run.

Athletes must concentrate, or stay "focused," on the race to come

Muscles in the upper arm and shoulder are used to pump the arms

A good start is vital in sprint races

Future sites

Organizing committees spend years preparing a bid for their city to host the games. The IOC tries to ensure that the games are spread around the world, so it does not award two consecutive games to the same country. Since 1992, the games have been awarded to North America, Australia, and Europe.

DEBORAH COMPAGNONI
One of the world's best slalom skiers of the 1990s, Deborah Compagnoni won gold medals at each of the three Olympic Games in the decade plus a silver in 1998. She will be aiming to continue her success in 2002 in Salt Lake City.

STARTING YOUNG
Young athletes who dream of becoming famous Olympians must be prepared for years of dedication and hard work. They will need talent and some good luck.

SUMMER SPORTS

Triathlete preparing for the cycle ride

SOFTBALL

TABLE TENNIS

TAE KWON DO

TENNIS

TRIATHLON

VOLLEYBALL
Beach volleyball
Volleyball

WEIGHT LIFTING

WRESTLING
Freestyle
Greco-Roman

TRIATHLON
A new Olympic sport in Sydney is the triathlon, in which athletes have to compete in three sports, one right after another. They swim 1.5 km (0.9 mile), cycle 40 km (25 miles), and run 10 km (6.2 miles). The first over the line wins. Any sport's international governing body can apply to be included in the games. If the sport meets certain conditions, it can be recognized as an Olympic sport.

ATHENS 2004
In 2004, the Olympic Games will return to the city where the modern games began in 1896. It has often been suggested that Athens should be the permanent site for the Summer Games because Greece was the home of the ancient Olympics.

The Acropolis of ancient Greece stands high above Athens

SALT LAKE CITY 2002
The eyes of the world will be on Salt Lake City when the Winter Games are held there in 2002. The city bid for the 1998 Winter Games too, but these were awarded to Nagano in Japan. The city tried again and spent millions of dollars in order to win the first Winter Games of the new millennium.

PARALYMPIC SUMMER SPORTS

There will be 18 sports at the Sydney 2000 Summer Paralympic Games.

ARCHERY

ATHLETICS

BASKETBALL

BOCCIE

CYCLING

EQUESTRIAN

FENCING

GOALBALL

JUDO

POWER LIFTING

RUGBY

SAILING

SHOOTING

SOCCER

SWIMMING

TABLE TENNIS

TENNIS

VOLLEYBALL

Rose Hill of Great Britain at Atlanta

WINTER SPORTS

There will be eight sports at the Salt Lake City 2002 Winter Games.

BIATHLON	SPEED SKATING
BOBSLED	SKIING
CURLING	Alpine
FIGURE SKATING	Freestyle
ICE HOCKEY	Nordic
LUGE	Snowboarding

PARALYMPIC WINTER SPORTS

Danja Haslacher of Austria at Nagano

There will be four sports at the Salt Lake City 2002 Winter Paralympic Games.

BIATHLON	SKIING
ICE-SLEDGE HOCKEY	Alpine
	Nordic
ICE-SLEDGE RACING	

Index

Acknowledgments

Dorling Kindersley would like to thank:
Athletes: Robert Earwicker (weight lifter), Rose Hill (paralympian), Kathy Read (swimmer), Anthony Sawyer (decathlete), Mary Sharman (dressage rider).

Model maker: Paul Fowler

Nutritionist: Jane Griffin

Designers of the Sydney Olympic Stadium: Bligh Lobb Sports Architecture

Index: Chris Bernstein

Picture Credits
The publishers would also like to thank the following for their kind permission to reproduce their photographs:

(a = above, b = below, c = center, l = left, r = right, t = top)

Action Plus: Chris Barry 27tr; Glyn Kirk 27br, 48bl, 55tr; Neil Tingle 26br, 42bl; Peter Sourrier 34tl; Tony Henshaw 33br.
AKG London: 14bc; Erich Lessing 9tr; John Hios 12bc, 13bc, 14tr, 14cr, 15cr; Musée du Louvre, Paris 30c; Olympia Museum 30cr.
Allsport: 17bc, 20cr, 21tl, 32cl, 33tl, 33bl, 34cl, 56cl; Agence Vandystadt/Bruno Bade 23br; Clive Brunskill 27tl, 27bl; Gary M Prior 17tr; Gray Mortimore 29tr, 29tl, 29tc, 29cr; Hulton Getty 19cr; IOC/Olympic Museum Collections 4l, 5bc, 6tl, 15br, 15tl, 16tr, 16bc, 16br, 17crr, 17cr, 17c, 17cl, 17cll, 17crrr, 17tl, 17bl, 18c, 18tr, 19tl, 19bl, 20tl, 22cl, 25tl, 34crb, 44c, 44b, 44-45t, 45b, 46ac, 46c, 46bc, 47br, 47bc, 47tr, 52tr, 52bl, 53bl, 55br, 55tl; John Gichigi 37tc; Michael Cooper 37tr; Mike Hewitt 22tr; Mike Powell 22br, 37cr, 47tc, 58cl; Nick Wilson 54cr; Pascal Rondeau 23tc, 26-27c; Shaun Botterill 26tr, 39tr; Simon Bruty 23cr, 26bl; SOCOG 21tr; Stephen Dunn 54br; Stu Forster 59br; Todd Warshaw 29bl; Tony Duffy 21br, 21cl.
Ancient Art & Architecture Collection: 8c, 11cr, 11bl, 13br, 13l, 16bl.
Associated Press: 54bl.
British Museum, London: 8bl, 9br, 10r, 10tl, 11tl, 11br, 16tl, 30-31b, 32tl, 43tr.
Colorsport: 31crb, 56cra, 58bl, 59tl.
Corbis UK Ltd.: 31cra.
Deutsches Archäologisches Institut, Berlin: 12c.
Empics Ltd.: Aubrey Washington 24bl, 31br.
E.T. Archive: 12tl, 18cl.
Mary Evans Picture Library: 10cl, 30tr.
Sonia Halliday Photographs: 8tr, 50cr.
Michael Holford: 10bl, 13tr.
Hulton Getty: 50tl, 53cr.
Imperial War Museum: 52c.

IOC/Olympic Museum Collections: 15bl, 25bl, 32bl, 33tr, 35tl, 43tc, 43c, 46-47tc, 50br, 51tl, 53br.
The Kobal Collection: Olympia-Film 32tr, 34bc, 35cr.
Popperfoto: 15tr, 20tc, 25c, 32br, 33bc, 34tr, 35bc, 52cr, 53t; Dave Joiner 25bc, 25abc.
Rex Features: Sipa Press 53cl, 54tr.
Roger-Viollet: 12bl, 12br, 14br.
Scala: Museo della Terme, Roma 9l.
Science Photo Library: David Ducros 55cr; Philippe Plailly/Eurelios 36bl.
Seiko Europe Ltd.: 50bl, 50cl, 51br, 51bc, 51cra, 51tr.
Sporting Pictures (UK) Ltd.: 35c.
Tony Stone Images: Chuck Pefley 58br; George Grigoriou 59bl.
Topham Picturepoint: 55bl.

Jacket:
Action Plus: Glyn Kirk front tr.
Allsport: IOC/Museum front bl, front cl, front cra, front crb; Mike Powell front c; Pascal Rondeau front bc.
Seiko Europe Ltd.: front br.

SUBJECTS

HISTORY

AFRICA

ANCIENT CHINA

ARMS & ARMOR

BATTLE

CASTLE

COWBOY

EXPLORER

KNIGHT

MEDIEVAL LIFE

MYTHOLOGY

NORTH AMERICAN INDIAN

PIRATE

PRESIDENTS

RUSSIA

SHIPWRECK

TITANIC

VIKING

WITCHES & MAGIC-MAKERS

ANCIENT WORLDS

ANCIENT EGYPT

ANCIENT GREECE

ANCIENT ROME

AZTEC, INCA & MAYA

BIBLE LANDS

MUMMY

PYRAMID

THE BEGINNINGS OF LIFE

ARCHEOLOGY

DINOSAUR

EARLY HUMANS

PREHISTORIC LIFE

THE ARTS

BOOK

COSTUME

DANCE

FILM

MUSIC

TECHNOLOGY

BOAT

CAR

FLYING MACHINE

FUTURE

INVENTION

SPACE EXPLORATION

TRAIN

PAINTING

GOYA

IMPRESSIONISM

LEONARDO & HIS TIMES

MANET

MONET

PERSPECTIVE

RENAISSANCE

VAN GOGH

WATERCOLOR

Future updates and editions will be available online at www.dk.com

DK EYEWITNESS BOOKS

A–Z

DK EYEWITNESS BOOKS

1–110

Future updates and editions will be available online at www.dk.com